TANKMASTER

A practical guide to setting up your
MARINE
TROPICAL AQUARIUM

DICK MILLS

INTERPET PUBLISHING

Author

Dick Mills, author of many aquarium books, is a former editor of The Aquarist & Pondkeeper magazine and also a Vice-President of the Federation of British Aquatic Societies. He has kept aquarium and pond fish continuously for the last 40 years, but also finds time to travel, when – as if by accident – he always manages to come across a public aquarium or two.

© 2001 Interpet Publishing,
Vincent Lane, Dorking, Surrey, RH4 3YX, England.
All rights reserved.
ISBN 13:978-1-903098-02-8
This reprint 2008

Credits

Created and designed: Ideas into Print,
New Ash Green, Kent DA3 8JD, England.
Production management: Consortium, Poslingford,
Suffolk CO10 8RA, England.
Print production: Sino Publishing House Ltd., Hong Kong.
Printed and bound in China.

Below: The smartly attired and elegant longnosed hawkfish (Oxycirrhites typus) is not a constantly active species. It is quite happy to perch on a rocky outcrop waiting for a passing 'meal' to pass by.

Contents

These flame angelfishes are typical of the dazzling colours seen in marine fishes.

Part One:

The marine aquarium is different

If your previous fishkeeping experience has been confined to tropical freshwater fish or pond fish, probably the biggest difference you will find when you start keeping marine fish (apart from the salt content of the water) is the fact that the number of marine fishes you can keep in an aquarium of any given size is far fewer than you may have been used to.

A second difference, especially with the basic marine setup, is the conspicuous absence of aquarium plants. Although decorative synthetic corals may be a reasonable substitute as a means of providing sanctuary for the fishes, they are nothing more than static objects. However, once you have gained some experience, you can progress from the simple marine aquarium described in these pages to the rather more complicated reef-type of aquarium. This will enable you to enjoy the more exciting living background provided by macro-algae, living corals and other invertebrate life.

The major impact of setting up a marine aquarium is that it places exacting responsibilities and disciplines on its owner. For reasons that will become apparent as you progress through this book, successful marine fishkeeping is in direct proportion to the amount of effort you are prepared to put into maintaining optimum conditions in the aquarium. If you are not prepared to dedicate yourself to regular tasks to ensure the well-being of the aquarium's inhabitants, you will be destined for disappointment.

However, all it is not doom and gloom, for although marine fishkeeping may be considered a relatively recent introduction within the fishkeeping hobby, there is much more pioneering work to be done, particularly in the area of captive breeding. Experience built upon the efforts of others in the past, together with the technological advances of modern aquarium equipment, have provided us with a much firmer foundation from which to advance. Every marine fishkeeper, regardless of their level of involvement, has something worthwhile to contribute.

Marine fishkeeping is no longer in the 'hit and miss' or 'try and hope' categories of years gone by. Modern air transportation systems ensure that livestock arrives in far better condition, aquarium equipment is completely reliable and there is a wider range of suitable aquarium foods available. And, of course, with the vast amount of information available in publications and on the Internet, both the experienced fishkeeper and the novice have a wealth of back-up information at their disposal.

Bringing the natural world into your home

Switch on the television or go on holiday to a sun-drenched island and the chances are that you will see (or be offered) an underwater journey on which you will encounter the brilliant colours and dazzling shoals of fish as they cruise around the coral reefs.

Modern day technology, while allowing you to view and visit such sights, also enables you to create a living souvenir in your own home. The fast jet transport that so effortlessly carried you away is also likely to be bringing thousands of fish to your aquatic dealer. No longer quite so dramatically stressed by the protracted journey, these living jewels are soon thriving in almost identical conditions to those of their native homes as they await your interest. But is it as easy as it sounds?

All it takes is to provide the fish with the same conditions as they would enjoy in nature – excellent water conditions, enough living space and a steady supply of nutritious foods. Fortunately, all the old problems encountered in the early days of marine fishkeeping have been resolved. Crucially, the ability to create synthetic seawater has removed the risk of introducing pathogens into the aquarium by using natural seawater. Modern equipment and practical knowledge make maintaining the water in optimum condition an easy task, while a greater appreciation of the lifestyle and needs of the animals themselves means that they will not be doomed to a short aquarium life as was the case in earlier times. A further encouragement (should you need one) is

Below: Delicate forms of soft corals cover the reef and provide shelter and perhaps food for many marine fishes. As your fishkeeping skills progress, maybe you will go on to create such a scene in a beautiful reef tank collection.

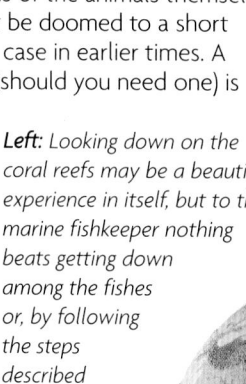

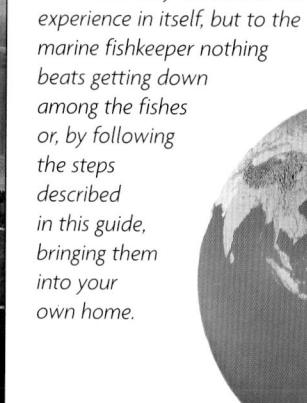

Left: Looking down on the coral reefs may be a beautiful experience in itself, but to the marine fishkeeper nothing beats getting down among the fishes or, by following the steps described in this guide, bringing them into your own home.

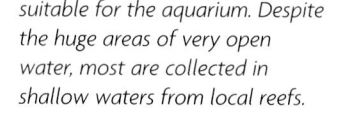

Left: The Indo-Pacific ocean is the natural home of a very large proportion of marine fishes suitable for the aquarium. Despite the huge areas of very open water, most are collected in shallow waters from local reefs.

that since most marine aquarium fishes are caught in shallow waters from coastal fringing reefs, the fishes that you enjoyed seeing in the wild will be readily available for your home aquarium, too.

If you add to these reassuring facts the existence of suitable aquarium materials well able to withstand the effect of proximity to corrosive seawater, then the possibility of a successful marine aquarium becomes a reality rather than a dream.

Although it is tempting to assume that recreating a coral reef in the home is within everyone's reach, remember that there is still a lot to learn before you can provide just the right environment in which the underwater panorama of your imagination will thrive. In this guide we introduce the delights of the marine aquarium in a restrained manner; we will establish a basic 'fish-only' collection from which you can gain worthwhile practical experience in marine aquarium management before deciding where your enthusiasm will take you next in the fishkeeping trail. Do not be

Above: The sandy texture of the seabed near a tropical reef not only harbours microscopic food, but can also provide sleeping accommodation for some marine fish species, such as this triggerfish, Balistapus undulatus.

Osmoregulation in marine fish

Because the fish is surrounded by saltwater, water constantly diffuses from its body. To maintain its salt content equilibrium, the fish drinks constantly but excretes little water.

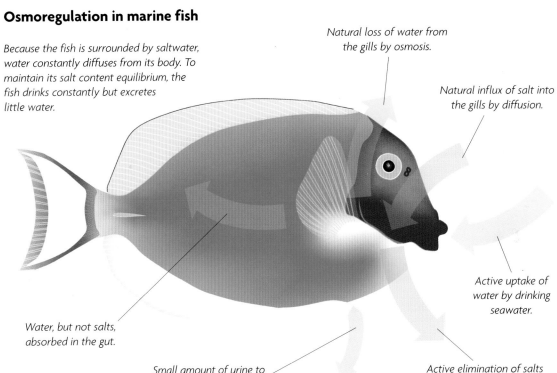

Natural loss of water from the gills by osmosis.

Natural influx of salt into the gills by diffusion.

Active uptake of water by drinking seawater.

Water, but not salts, absorbed in the gut.

Small amount of urine to conserve body fluid.

Active elimination of salts by chloride cells in the gills.

too impatient; your fishes' lives are at stake here. Help them by creating the proper aquarium conditions and they will repay your efforts by displaying all their varying colours and fascinating behaviour right before your eyes.

However, the marine aquarium does not just provide a window through which to view the underwater world. It is far from being just an animated decorative feature for your living room.

By keeping, caring for and observing the fishes in your aquarium, you could be making a contribution to their conservation. The more we know about the animals in our charge, the more we can perhaps replicate their needs for captive culture. In this way, we could reduce the need to catch them from the wild, denuding their natural homes and, at the very least, sparing them the long flights that, no doubt, they find as exhausting and tedious as we do.

The factor that really boosted support for marine fishkeeping was the introduction of the all-glass aquarium. Before this, the only option was a traditional angle-iron frame with glass panels set in putty. Inevitably, the corrosive effect of the saltwater damaged the frame and severely reduced the life of the aquarium. However, silicone-sealed, all-glass tanks proved to be completely impervious to such damage and since their introduction, the marine aquarium has never looked back. Nowadays, acrylic aquariums moulded (or extruded) in one piece are also available. Commercially available tanks should conform to industry standards with regard to the thickness of glass required for the volume of water to be contained. Although it is possible to make your own tanks, you should understand this important factor before you undertake such a task.

Tanks can be almost any shape and can be tailored to suit almost any space: oblongs, cubes, 'L' or triangular shapes designed to fit around or into corners are all viable. The main thing is to ensure that whatever shape tank you decide to install, it has the largest water surface area possible. Absolute water volume (including deep tanks) has little bearing on the number of fish a tank will hold. Indeed, deep tanks are often more difficult to manage than the normal 'standard depth' aquariums.

As the water conditions in the marine aquarium need to be at their absolute best at all times, it makes sense to opt for the largest aquarium your space (and finances) can accommodate from the very outset. Firstly (and most importantly), a relatively large volume of water will provide more

Fish length and water surface

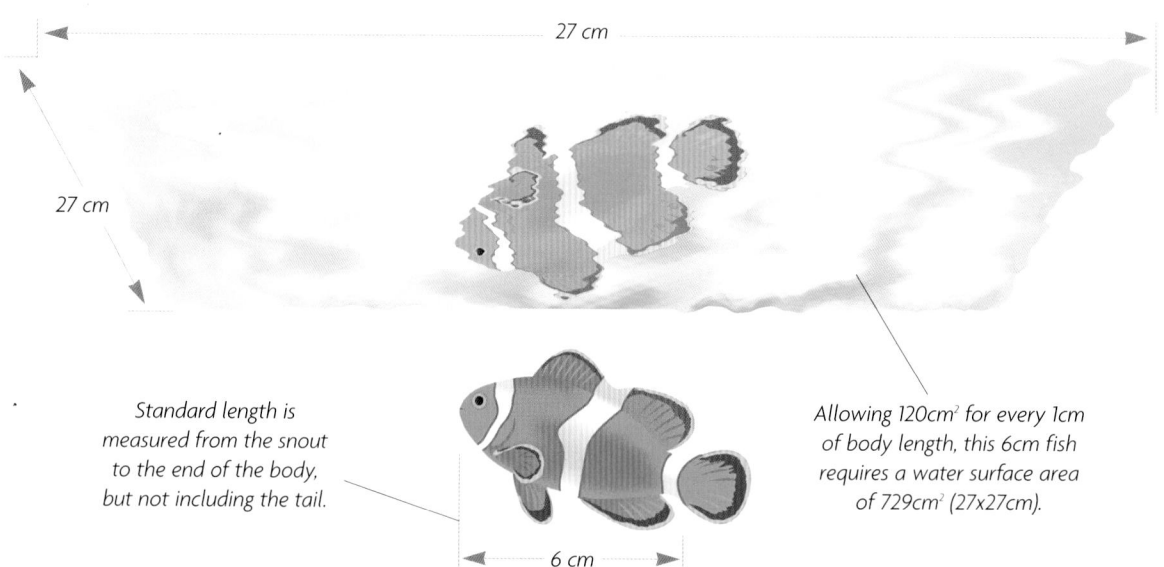

27 cm

27 cm

Standard length is measured from the snout to the end of the body, but not including the tail.

6 cm

Allowing 120cm² for every 1cm of body length, this 6cm fish requires a water surface area of 729cm² (27x27cm).

stable conditions over a longer period than a smaller aquarium. Secondly, because the number of tropical marine fish that can be kept is much smaller than the number of coldwater or tropical freshwater species in the same volume of water, a larger aquarium will at least ensure that you have a reasonable number of the fish to look at.

To house an adequate display of fishes, choose an aquarium at least 90cm (36in) long by 38cm (15in) high by 30cm (12in) front to back. Because you must maintain optimum water conditions at all times, you

should incorporate a fully-filtered system and, for the basic aquarium set up, this means an external canister filter providing mechanical, chemical and biological functions, together with protein skimming. As long as the aquarium is not stocked with too many fish, the light bioload should not be beyond the capability of this basic system.

In a 90x38x30cm (36x15x12in) aquarium, applying the guide of 120cm² of water surface per centimetre of fish body length (excluding the tail) we arrive at its total fish holding capacity of 23cm (9in) of 'fish'.

(This is equivalent to 1in of fish length per 48in² of tank surface area.) Of course, you cannot interpret this total literally, as a single 23cm (9in)-long fish would not look very impressive in a 90cm (36in)-long tank. Neither would 23 one centimetre-long (0.4in) fishes be the answer for, even if they were to be available at this size, their oxygen requirements and waste disposal needs would simply increase as they grew, presenting you with even more problems. The answer is to find a compromise, progressively building up fish stocks over several months to enable the filtration system to cope with the increasing bioload – and allowing you to cope with the cost!

Below: A fantastic reef aquarium such as this may be every marine fishkeeper's dream, but consider just how large – and therefore heavy – it is. It needs supporting on substantial piers. Make sure that even a tank of more modest proportions is set up on a base that is firm, level and strong.

What you will need

Setting up a marine aquarium isn't something you can do on the spur of the moment; it is going to take time, money and patience. Draw up a plan of action and make sure you have all the equipment you need to hand before you start. Examine individual items of equipment before you install them to make sure they are complete and that you understand how they work. Read the manufacturer's instructions and allow plenty of time for the actual setting up process. Here is a shopping list of items you will need to set up the tank described in this book.

Stand to suit the size of aquarium (or cabinet to suit)
Piece of plywood (same size as stand top/tank base)
Polystyrene sheet (same size as stand top/tank base)
Tank (90cm/36in minimum length)
Heater-thermostat units (2)
Substrate material (two bucketsful)
Plastic bowl and bucket
Salt mix (enough for 110 litres/ 24 gallons)
Thermometer
Hydrometer

Decor (rocks, barnacles, replica corals)
Protein skimmer
Pump (for protein skimmer)
External filter (including media)
Reflector/hood
Fluorescent tube(s)
Starter gear
Condensation tray/cover glass
Airstones
Airpump
Airline tubing
Aquarium background
Multi-outlet power socket
Cable tidy (optional)

Tools:

Spirit level
Small adjustable spanner
Scissors
Craft knife
Pliers
Insulating tape
Methylated spirit
Polishing cloth
Spatula
Rubber gloves (for use with testing kits)
Hosepipe for filling tank

STAGE 1 Setting up the tank

Before you set up an aquarium anywhere in the house, there are a number of important factors to consider if it is to function correctly, safely and satisfy your requirements.

Firstly, bear in mind that a set-up aquarium is very heavy. An aquarium measuring 90x38x30cm (36x15x12in) will hold about 110 litres (24 gallons) of water, weighing approximately 100 kg (over 220 lb). It will be impossible to move once it is full of water, substrate and decor, so make absolutely sure you are satisfied with its location before proceeding to set it up. It needs to be supported on a very firm and level foundation; a conveniently vacant bookcase or

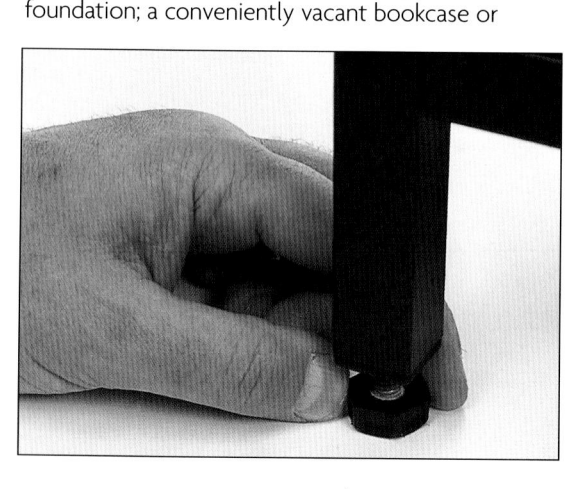

Above: *Most aquarium stands are supplied with adjustable 'levelling' feet. Once in position, make sure the stand is level in all directions – left to right and front to back. Make final adjustments with the empty tank in position.*

bureau top will not do. If you are installing an aquarium in an upstairs location, ensure that its weight is evenly distributed across any floor supports, not between them.

Because the aquarium will require electricity, it makes sense to position the aquarium near a power outlet. Although it also needs light, this does not mean it has to be near a window. Strict control of the amount of light entering the aquarium is vital if you are to avoid problems with unsightly algae growths. As the aquarium needs to be heated, it makes sense to place it in an area with a relatively stable temperature – neither adjacent to a draughty doorway, nor near a window where summer sunshine would overheat the water. Bearing in mind the need for regular partial water changes, the water supply (and also the means to dispose of water) should be near at hand if at all possible.

The tank must be level, not only so that the waterline is straight when viewed from the front, but also to ensure that the water pressure on the glass panels is evenly spread. Use the levelling feet on the aquarium stand to compensate for irregularities in the flooring and make a further check, using the top frames of the tank as a guide.

With the stand in place and level, place a sheet of wood on top, followed by a sheet of polystyrene or plastic foam. This acts as a cushion between the aquarium and the wood surface and absorbs any irregularities that may otherwise stress the glass base.

Although a metal stand certainly provides a means of supporting the tank in its chosen position, you may want to go a bit further and invest in a custom-made cabinet in which to house the tank. This has the added advantage that most of the necessary external 'hardware', such as filtration equipment, can be hidden from view, leaving only the decorative aquarium on display. If you do decide to 'cabinet-install,' make sure you can access the tank easily for regular maintenance purposes.

Cleaning the tank

It pays to clean the aquarium thoroughly before setting it up and you can do this fairly conveniently once it is in its final position. You will find that aquarium accessories attached by 'sucker caps' stick much better to clean glass. First remove any packaging tapes, fingermarks and so on. Wash the inside of the tank with warm, slightly salty water and dry it off with a lint-free cloth or paper towel. A final polish with a cloth soaked in methylated spirits will remove any stubborn grease or packaging adhesive. Polish the outside of the glass with proprietary glass cleaner if you wish – but never the inside!

Levelling the tank

Make the final levelling check with the tank in place. It must be perfectly level to avoid setting up stresses in the glass panels when it is filled with water. Remember that it is impossible to make levelling adjustments once the tank is full.

Check the level of the tank in both directions. The tank is cushioned on a polystyrene sheet to even out imperfections in the wooden base.

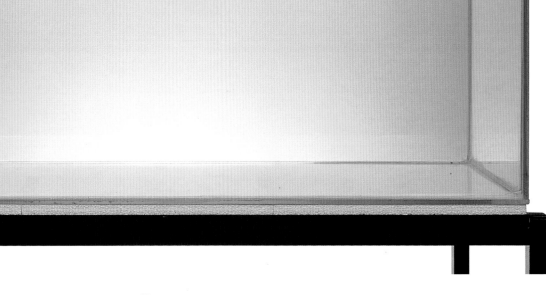

STAGE 2 *Preparing and adding the substrate*

The function of the substrate layer in marine aquariums is slightly different from that in freshwater tanks in that it does not support rooted plant growth. Until fairly recently, its main purpose was to act as a biological filtration medium for nitrifying bacteria and as a home for any burrowing fish and invertebrates. Today, this form of filtration has been

Right: Burrowing fish, such as this yellow-faced jawfish (Opisthognathus aurifrons) require a reasonable depth of substrate (say 7.5cm/3in) in which to tunnel.

Below: Substrate material needs thorough cleaning before it is added to the aquarium. Wash about a third of a bucketful at a time. Repeat the rinsing until the water runs clear. Use a light-coloured bucket to help you see what is happening.

superseded by more modern methods, so there is no longer any need to provide sufficient substrate for filtration purposes.

The majority of modern marine aquariums incorporate just a thin layer of substrate for decorative purposes, while the biological filtration functions are performed outside the aquarium. Thicker, deeper layers of substrate are used in tanks (or even in a separate 'sump' tank), where alternative water treatment is housed (see page 49). The danger of deep, undisturbed substrates is that they may turn into anaerobic (oxygen-starved) areas that produce hydrogen sulphide. They also encourage unwanted algal growths.

Substrate materials generally consist of crushed coral and coral sand. Aragonite sand, which is rich in dissolvable calcium carbonate, is a popular choice.

Usually, all substrate materials are calcareous in some form, which helps to maintain the necessary high pH values (about 8.3).

Before using any substrate material, be sure to wash it thoroughly. Fill a bucket about a third full and run a hose into it. If you can do this over a water disposal pipe, you can continually stir the material until the run-off water remains clear. Alternatively you may have to 'hand-wash' each small volume, pouring off any dirty water from time to time until you reach the 'clean' stage.

Place each cleaned batch of substrate material into the aquarium and spread it evenly over the base. Sometimes it looks effective to make a slight downward slope from the back towards the front of the aquarium, but water and fish movements soon 'flatten' out all your good artistic intentions!

Adding the substrate

Cover the whole of the base of the aquarium with about 1cm (0.4in) of substrate material. There should be enough material to support the rocks so that they do not sit directly on the bottom glass.

Caution

From this point on, you will be working in and around the tank installing various items. Keep checking that the tank hasn't moved on its base as it will be impossible to correct this later on when the tank is full of heavy objects and water!

STAGE 3 Adding heaters

Of all the essential technical requirements in a marine aquarium, heating is the easiest to fit and the least demanding to maintain. A simple, thermostatically controlled electric immersion heater hangs in the tank and switches itself on and off as needed. In tanks over 60cm (24in) long, it is usual to divide the total wattage of heat required into two, and install two heaters, one at each end of the tank. As well as ensuring an even spread of heat, you can be reassured that if one of the heaters should fail, the other will act as a back-up.

Heaters are wired into the electricity supply, usually through a 'cable tidy' connecting box. Unlike pumps and lights, they are NOT serviced by switched circuits. When carrying out maintenance within the aquarium, switch off the power supply at the power outlet before putting your hands into the tank. Allow some minutes to elapse following 'switch off' to allow any residual heat in the heaters to expend itself before you work on the tank, especially if it is to be drained of water.

Fitting heaters is an easy task; simply attach their supporting suction caps to the glass of the aquarium. To ensure long-lasting suction, fix the suckers to the dry glass before adding the water. As the water is added, it will increase the pressure on the suckers. Fitting suction caps under water is not so successful, as there is always a small amount of water trapped between the suction cap and glass that minimises the cling-on effect.

Always make sure that heaters are mounted clear of the substrate material to allow maximum circulation of water around the heater. If the heater is allowed to lie on the surface of the substrate, local boiling action could occur, with the result that the glass tube containing the heater element may crack. Similarly, do not crowd tank decorations around the heater unit or otherwise restrict water movement around it.

There are other methods of heating the water. Some external canister power filter units have heating elements incorporated into their design. Where the filtration system is made up of a separate sump unit, often housed immediately below the aquarium, heaters may be placed in the sump rather than in the aquarium itself.

To adjust the water temperature, simply turn the control at the top of the heater-thermostat unit. A quarter turn is the most you will need in any direction to effect a change. Allow at least 30-60 minutes to elapse before re-reading the water temperature. The action of the heater is generally indicated by a small neon lamp within the heater body; when it is lit, you know that the heater is working.

Do not confuse the heater's 'temperature-set' indicator with the actual temperature of the water — always check the thermometer in or on the tank.

Right: Sometimes fishes, especially those of a nervous disposition, may attempt to shelter too near a heater, with the result that they may suffer burns. Heater guards can be fitted around the heater units to prevent this occurring.

What size heater to fit?

Allow about 10 watts per 4.54 litres (1 gallon) of water content. Our 90x30x38cm (36x15x12in) aquarium has an approximate volume of 110 litres (24 gallons) and would therefore require 240 watts of heat. A smaller-sized heater would be sufficient if the room is permanently heated. Following the guidelines described above, a single 250-watt heater should suffice, but two separate 150-watt heaters would be better and afford some margin for error or heater failure.

Positioning the heaters

Place one heater at each end of the aquarium above the substrate. This helps to spread the heat around the aquarium more effectively and provides a standby if one heater should fail. Always keep a spare heater-thermostat handy in case of failures.

Safety first

NEVER switch on heaters unless they are under water – they can heat up very quickly!

Fix the heaters at an angle, with the heating element at the bottom, so that as the heat rises it does not bypass the thermostat. Read the instructions supplied with each unit, as designs and instructions may vary.

STAGE 4 Installing a protein skimmer

Because the breakdown of organic substances in the aquarium leads to pollution of the water (especially in the subsequent production of algae-encouraging nitrates) it makes sense to remove these as soon as possible. One of the physical properties of organic compounds is that they stick to any junctions between air and water, such as the surface film around air bubbles in the aquarium water. If it were possible to create a suitable interface in the tank, it should be a simple process to collect organic matter from it and dispose of it.

Protein skimmers make use of this affinity by creating a mass of bubbles in a column of water contained in a cylinder with an overflow facility at its top. To maximise the collection of organic matter, the aquarium water must be exposed to the column of bubbles for the maximum period of time. In the most modern protein skimmers, this is achieved by arranging the water flow through the skimmer to run in the opposite direction to the rising mass of bubbles – this is known as a 'countercurrent' design.

Protein skimmers may be air-operated (using an airstone) or be fed by a water pump connected to a venturi device that creates the bubbles. (A venturi is simply a pipe with an internal restriction that speeds up the flow of water and reduces its pressure. At this point in the pipe there is an air intake and the reduced water pressure sucks in a flow of air to produce a swirling mass of bubbles.)

In either case, a collecting cup sits on top of the cylinder body into which the organic-laden froth overflows and from where it can be periodically emptied. Immediately after the protein skimmer is

Foam settling chamber

Air intake for venturi

Twin water return tubes to the aquarium

Water input from pump in the aquarium

Adjustable bracket to locate protein skimmer over the aquarium top shelf.

Square base rests against the aquarium glass and maintains the unit in vertical position.

Anatomy of a protein skimmer

Protein-laden foam overflows into this cup and settles out into a discardable liquid.

Cleaned water returns to the aquarium from the outer cylinder of the skimmer.

Air drawn into the venturi creates a mass of bubbles in the water flow.

Air bubbles rising up the central tube attract protein from the water. The foam progresses upwards, while the cleaned water continues its longer path towards the outlet.

installed and before any fish are added to the tank, there will be little organic matter to dispose of. When emptying any collected organic material from the collecting cup, it is a good idea to clean the internal surfaces of the skimmer column, thus removing any accumulated fatty materials that would lessen the water surface tension and restrict the skimmer's efficiency. The constant removal of organic compounds is made even further complete by performing regular partial water changes of, say, 20%-25%. (See routine maintenance, page 54.)

As with the heating apparatus, the protein skimmer can be installed within the aquarium or in a separate sump. In our example, the skimmer is an external 'hang-on' model. Because the action of the protein skimmer takes place in an enclosed container within the aquarium or alongside it, it is often convenient to use it in conjunction with ozone. (It is vital to isolate this dangerous oxidising gas from the livestock in the aquarium.) The use of ozone in the marine aquarium is discussed in more detail on page 45.

Right: Once the aquarium has become established, organic matter will be separated from the water by the protein skimmer and deposited in the collecting cup.

Connecting the pump

Hang the skimmer onto the back pane of the tank and connect it to a separate submersible water pump in the aquarium. Keep the pump inlet clear from obstructing decorations.

Fit the output tube from the water pump firmly to the skimmer intake pipe.

STAGE 5 Installing an external filter

The prime objective of filtration is not merely to keep the water crystal clear so that you can see your fish, but to cleanse the water thoroughly of any toxic materials and other pollutants that might endanger their lives while they are in your care.

The external canister filter effectively deals with any suspended debris in the aquarium water. Within the canister are various filter media, each designed to perform a specific function, as explained here.

To prevent undue disturbance of the aquarium, the returning water from the filter can be distributed across the aquarium (just below the surface) by means of a spraybar. This will set up water currents and produce beneficial agitation at the surface to help oxygen diffuse into the water and carbon dioxide to disperse. Alternatively, a single return jet may be used, its power being tempered by directing its output into the corner of the tank. In this case, the inlet tube to the filter should be positioned at the other end of the aquarium to create water flow right across the aquarium. Whichever method of return is used, it is vital not to allow aquarium decorations to block the flow of water to the filter inlet tube, no matter how desirable it is to disguise its presence with a convenient rock or two.

The advantage of having an external filter with isolating 'taps' is that you can shut it off from the aquarium for cleaning purposes without disturbing the aquarium's inmates or decorations in any way. Reconnecting the filter after cleaning, opening the taps and switching on the power is all that is needed to restart the filtration system. Although internal filters can be used, they take up valuable swimming space in the aquarium and are less convenient to maintain, as they need to be removed from the tank for cleaning – a process that may disturb the decor and stress the fish at the same time.

The combination of external filtration coupled with protein skimming is now the accepted norm for the basic marine aquarium and one that we follow in this guide.

Filter media

This filter floss traps any small particles, giving the water a final polish before it returns to the tank.

Activated carbon adsorbs chemical compounds and any yellow coloration.

Filter floss 'separator'

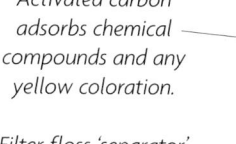

Ceramic pieces harbour colonies of aerobic bacteria that 'purify' the water.

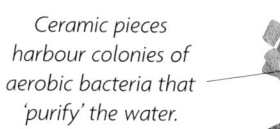

This block of sponge holds back any large particles in the flow.

An external canister filter

These plastic tubes carry water to and from the aquarium.

Shut-off taps allow you to disconnect the filter without water spillage.

The electric water pump is housed in the top part of the filter.

The incoming water passes upwards through the filter media, packed in a plastic basket inside the canister. Water flow must be maintained at all times to prevent the media turning anaerobic (without oxygen), as would occur within a short time following any failure of the power supply.

Fitting the pipework

This pipe returns cleaned water from the external canister filter located beneath the aquarium.

Right: Fit the spraybar along the back glass just beneath the water surface. Align the outlet holes to direct water across the upper water level at assist gaseous exchange.

This is the intake pipe for water being drawn from the aquarium and passing to the external filter. Keep the end of the pipe clear of the substrate.

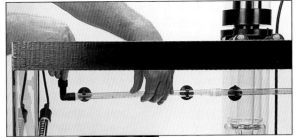

STAGE 6 *Adding decor*

Aquarium decor gives the fishes a sense of security, sanctuary and also delineates their territories. At the same time, it hides the tank 'hardware' and makes the whole underwater scene look more natural.

There is a wide range of materials to choose from but, aesthetic tastes apart, the most important factor to bear in mind is not to use any material that may leach out harmful substances into the water or otherwise affect its composition.

Pieces of rock are popular items of decoration. Choose these carefully, as their mineral composition may upset the water conditions. Reject any rocks that have visible veins of metallic deposits, no matter how attractive or unusual they may seem. Many calcium-based rocks, however, will be of benefit in the marine aquarium, and tufa rock, with its many porous internal passageways, can also assist biological filtration by offering homes to literally millions of bacteria.

In recent years, the use of skeletal remains of corals as decoration has been discouraged in the light of conservation issues. However, extremely realistic replicas have become available that are made from resins that are inert, safe to use and look much like the authentic article.

It is possible to build up a 'wall' of rock against the rear wall of the aquarium – some pieces of rock can be encouraged to lodge together by using a dab of two or aquarium sealant – but avoid creating 'dead areas' where little water movement occurs or where a fish can become trapped, usually unseen by the hobbyist. Rocky caves can also be created using the 'build-and-glue' technique. As previously mentioned,

water flow (and also maintenance-necessary access) to the aquarium hardware should not be impeded.

Be sure to clean every piece of aquarium decor before use, especially any from a natural marine source that may still be harbouring remnants of previous inhabitants (except 'live rock', see page 44). Soaking for a long period in successive changes of clean water will eventually clean the decoration. If in doubt, use your nose to test for impurities!

Although aquarium decoration is a matter of taste, try to emulate nature as far as possible. Artificial 'barnacles' or clamshells look better in a group rather than scattered separately. Similarly, build up rock formations using similar types of rock – with strata lines running correctly! To make things look even more natural, fine material made by crushing some of the rocks used and sprinkled on the substrate surface will blend rocks and substrate together.

Rocks for a marine aquarium

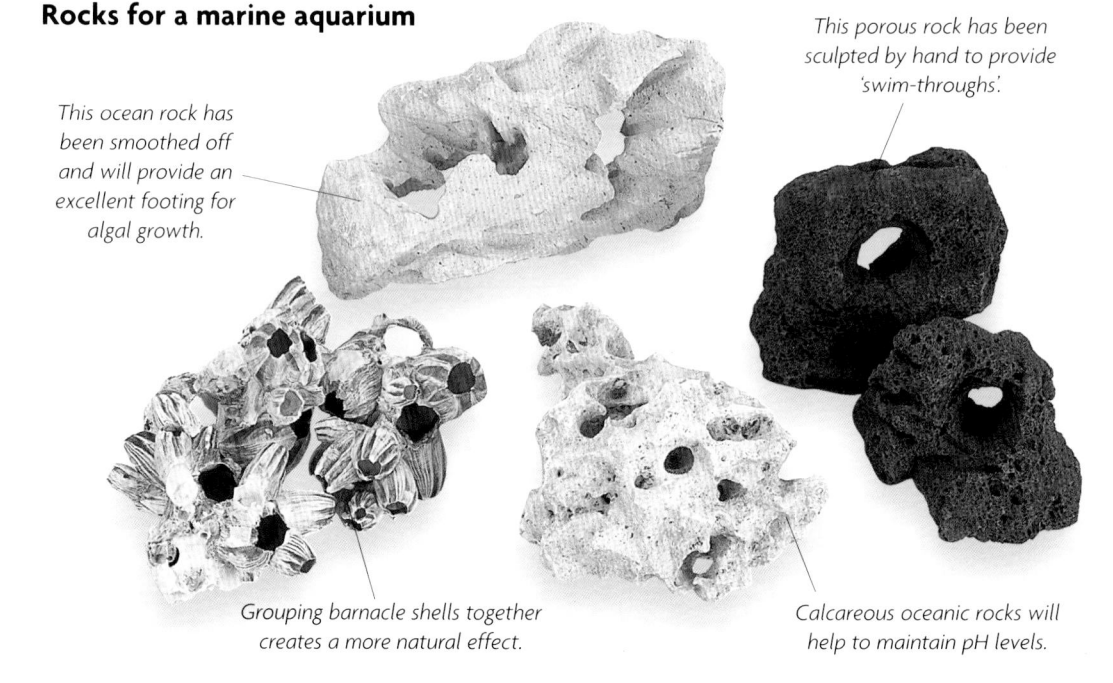

This ocean rock has been smoothed off and will provide an excellent footing for algal growth.

This porous rock has been sculpted by hand to provide 'swim-throughs'.

Grouping barnacle shells together creates a more natural effect.

Calcareous oceanic rocks will help to maintain pH levels.

Positioning rocks in the tank

Place the rocks carefully one by one to avoid damaging the tank glass or aquarium hardware.

You can glue 'piled up' rocks together with aquarium sealant to stop them toppling over.

Make sure that the heaters are clear of the substrate and have adequate water flow around them.

STAGE 7 Adding water and salt

Fortunately for the marine aquarist, the majority of marine fishes all come from waters with a very similar composition, unlike freshwater species, which can originate in many different types of water. This simplifies the challenge of providing saltwater of the correct quality.

Seawater has a general 'saltiness' of about 35 parts per thousand (35 ppt), but this is not the usual value used to express the correct strength of seawater as used in the aquarium. Instead, the unit of Specific Gravity (S.G.) is used to describe the ratio of density between sea and freshwater, and is measured with a special hydrometer. The correct S.G. for our tank is 1.022, a value indicated on the hydrometer's scale, which is also calibrated for use at the optimum water temperature (24°C/75°F) that we shall be using.

To provide the correct type of saltwater, we use proprietary salt mixes that are readily available from the aquatic store and simply mixed with tapwater. Many marine fishkeepers treat the tapwater first in order to remove or neutralise chlorine, chloramines and any heavy metals. Others prefer to start with purer forms of water, such as deionised or R.O. (Reverse Osmosis) water (see page 47).

When you fill the aquarium for the very first time, you will be dealing with a considerable volume of water and you might think that you will need a container approaching the size of a bath to mix in the salt. However, if you pause to think for a minute, you will realise that the aquarium itself makes the ideal mixing receptacle. Subsequently, you will only be adding relatively small amounts of water when you carry out regular partial water changes. You can prepare these mixes in a non-metallic bucket. Do not add any salt to the aquarium until you have turned on the heating and the water temperature has reached 24°C (75°F).

How much salt will you need?

You could decide to do things the hard way – measure volumes of water, calculate the weight of salt needed – but the easiest way is to buy a pack of salt mix that most closely equates to the volume of your aquarium. Most salt mixes are bagged up to make up specific volumes of seawater, so you need an approximate idea of how much water your aquarium holds. Reduce this value slightly to allow for displacement by substrate and tank decorations, but add a bit for external filtration systems.

Below: Use the aquarium to prepare the initial seawater mix. Add the freshwater first. By directing the water onto a piece of rock you avoid disturbing the substrate.

Gently add salt to the water in the aquarium. Turn on the filtration system to provide water flow and assist mixing. Place two airstones in the aquarium for additional aeration.

Turn on the aquarium heating. Do not add the salt until the water has reached the required temperature, 24°C (75°C).

25

STAGE 8 Creating the correct specific gravity

Continue to add water until the aquarium is almost full. This way you can put your hands and arms into the tank to move decorations around (to hide the hardware) and make adjustments to the hardware (return spraybar, water pump speed for the protein skimmer) without causing the tank to overflow. Turn on the aquarium heating, as well as the external filter, and add two airstones to increase aeration. At this point you can add any water treatments, such as dechlorinators. Once the water has reached the correct temperature, add the required amount of salt and allow it to dissolve. The water movement caused by the filter assists the dissolving process and the extra aeration quickly dissipates any build-up of carbon dioxide, as well as helping to re-aerate the water. Now take your first hydrometer reading to establish the specific gravity.

No-one is going to get things right at the first attempt; without any doubt, values will be over or under what you expect. The first reading of the hydrometer will show if less or more salt mix is needed. If the reading is slightly below the required

Initial water quality

Not all domestic water supplies are of the same composition and some may need treating to remove pollutants before you mix in any salt. There are a number of preparations available from your aquatic retailer to render the water safe. They are easy to use; simply add them to the water in the tank before you put in the salt. Follow the manufacturer's directions.

Storing salt mix

If you do buy more salt mix than you need for your aquarium, reseal the bag and store it in a cool, dry place for future use.

Do not be concerned that you may make too much sea water at once. Even if you do (and manage to get the S.G. spot on at the same time) you can keep any surplus water for use at the first water change.

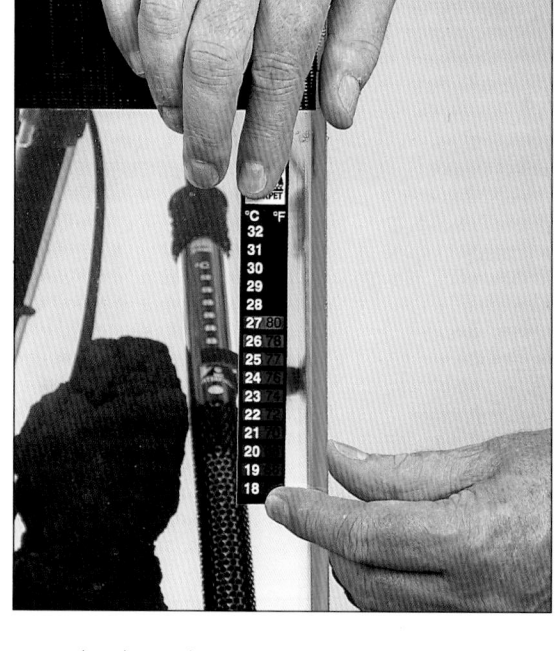

Right: *Easy-to-read external liquid crystal thermometers won't bob around the tank and end up out of convenient sight as floating types do.*

value, add more salt, bearing in mind that you will be adding more water to 'top up' the tank, which will further reduce the value in the process. Leave the tank for some time – say one hour – for the salt to dissolve before taking another S.G. reading. When you are satisfied with the final arrangement of decor and equipment in the tank, top it up with water and take another reading.

If the S.G. reading is too high after the final topping up, remove a proportion of the saltwater and replace it with freshwater to bring the value down to the required figure. If the reading is too low, add more salt. After making any addition of salt or dilutions with freshwater, always give the aquarium time to settle down before taking a new reading. Once the water in the tank has reached the required

S.G. value, leave the aquarium for at least 24 hours to allow the salt to be completely mixed and all the carbon dioxide to escape. At this stage, you can remove any additional aeration if you wish.

Once the tank conditions have stabilised following the salt mixing, turn on the protein skimmer. There will be little evidence of its operation until there is sufficient organic matter in the aquarium for it to collect, a function not likely to be seen until well after the addition of the first livestock.

Adjusting the specific gravity

The principle of the hydrometer is that it sinks lower or floats higher to reflect the density of the water. Aquarium hydrometers are calibrated to reflect specific gravity at the normal tank temperature of 24°C (75°F). The correct S.G. is indicated when the chosen value coincides with the miniscus (water surface level). It is easy to see in a coloured section on the stem.

1 If you take a test before adding any salt to the aquarium, the hydrometer will float very low, a clear indication that the specific gravity is far too low.

Correct 'range' of specific gravity

Some hydrometers also have built-in thermometers.

2 Adding salt will make the water 'denser', but do not take the reading until all the salt has dissolved. During this time you will notice the hydrometer rising in the water.

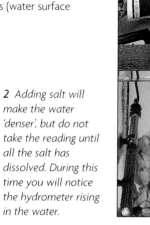

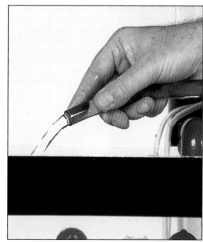

3 If you add too much salt, top up the tank with freshwater to reduce the 'too high' S.G. reading. If the tank is already full, siphon out some water and replace it with fresh until you obtain the correct reading.

4 A quick glance at this combined hydrometer/ thermometer tells you that both the S.G. and temperature are correct.

How specific gravity varies with temperature

Specific gravity is the ratio between the density of salt and freshwater. But density fluctuates with changes in temperature (decreasing as the temperature rises), so it is important to use a hydrometer calibrated for aquarium temperatures.

STAGE 9 *Fitting a condensation tray*

A condensation tray, or cover glass, is important for three reasons. Firstly, it prevents any condensation forming inside the hood, which would damage the light fittings, and it collects salt deposits from any spray thrown up by aeration or water surface turbulence. Thirdly, it provides an escape deterrent to fish, many of which are excellent jumpers.

The problem with all reflector/hoods and condensation trays is that most are incompatible with any hardware! There is always a cable, pipe or fixing bracket that must be accommodated at tank-top level, which inevitably means some serious physical modification to the hood and condensation tray. Fortunately, the materials used for hood and condensation tray construction are thin and can be cut with sturdy scissors or tin-snips. Be aware when cutting the hood that modifications may weaken its integrity; this is important, because it will need to house the starter gear for the fluorescent lighting.

Another problem can arise with internal hardware. The moulded-on electrical plugs supplied with most aquarium equipment may not pass through the small gap between the glass supporting shelves around the top of the tank. Cutting the cable and refitting a substitute plug (after passing the cable through the gap) is easy enough, but make sure you do not invalidate any manufacturer's guarantees.

If your tank does not conform to a standard size – perhaps it was specially made to suit your available space – you may have to modify the condensation trays available at your aquatic store. You may need to buy two and overlap them, after removing a 'side-end' from each. Alternatively, you could make your own cover glasses from separate pieces of glass or clear polycarbonate. Again, these can slide over each other to allow for easy access to the tank for feeding and maintenance. Some 'ready-made' condensation trays have built-in access doors for feeding.

Even if you opt for a pendant light over the tank, you will still require a condensation tray or cover glass, for the reasons outlined above. Whatever the condensation tray is made of, keep it scrupulously .clean at all times. Remove any build-up of green algae (the moist underside of condensation trays is an ideal algae-growing zone). Try dropping a few scrapings into the tank for the benefit of any herbivores present.

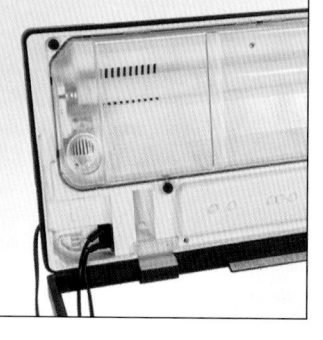

Left: Lighting tubes are completely safeguarded against moisture damage by virtue of the 'sealed in' construction of this reflector/hood. They can be replaced easily as needed.

An alternative cover glass

Two separate sheets of glass sliding in double channelling make for easy aquarium access.

Use silicone sealant to attach glass marbles as handles.

Simply slide back one sheet of glass to feed the fish.

When you have made any necessary modifications to the condensation tray, fit it into place.

Be sure to keep condensation trays free of algae, so that the maximum amount of light can pass through into the aquarium.

STAGE 10 Adding fluorescent lighting

For the aquarium to function both decoratively and as a home for the fishes, it requires light. For simple viewing purposes, a single fluorescent tube should suffice and you can choose the 'hue', or colour spectrum, you prefer. In a simple fish-only marine aquarium there will be little plant life requiring strong lighting to activate photosynthesis, and a lack of over-strong lighting should help to keep unsightly algal growths down to a minimum.

To achieve an even light across the aquarium, the fluorescent tube should occupy as much of the length of the reflector/hood as possible. Modern hoods are designed to accommodate a 90cm (36in)-long tube on a 90cm (36in) aquarium. As fluorescent tubes remain relatively cool, there is no build-up of

heat within the hood, nor any risk of the surface layers of the water becoming overheated.

Fluorescent lighting requires 'starter gear' that is accommodated in a compartment at the rear of the hood. This equipment is very heavy, so always remove the hood carefully when maintaining the aquarium, as a dropped starter gear could easily smash the tank. In the interests of safety, always use waterproof connectors with the tubes. Some hoods have a built-in waterproof sealed lighting unit as protection against water splashes and spray.

The intensity of the light from a single tube can be enhanced in a number of ways. At the very least, the interior of the hood should be white, but it could be lined with metal foil to reflect even more light (but do not block up any ventilation holes).

You will need to add more fluorescent tubes if you wish to encourage the growth of macro-algae for the benefit of herbivorous fishes. As a second tube, many fishkeepers choose an 'actinic' type, which gives the aquarium a blue-moon colour cast. Although our tank will be invertebrate-free, such lighting will be of more benefit to reef tanks containing live soft corals, which fluoresce under this particular blue spectrum.

Left: Fitting water-proof connectors to the fluorescent tube makes sense, as electricity and water make a dangerous combination. Make sure the pins line up with the holes before attempting to slide on the connector.

In some fluorescent lamps the visible output centres around a specific colour spectrum; freshwater aquarists will be familiar with lamps designed to assist optimum plant growth and enhance the red colours of the fish. Very often, combining a 'warm white' tube with a 'northlight' or 'daylight' tube will provide just the colour lighting you are trying to achieve.

With 'multi-tubes' fitted into the hood, you may wish to operate the lighting using a separate time switch for each lamp, so that the lighting simulates the build-up of natural daylight, or to provide separate viewing 'moods' depending on time of day.

Bear in mind that the efficiency of fluorescent lamps declines as the months pass. Renew the lamps at least once a year. Some tubes have a built-in 'fail-time'. They continue to produce almost full brilliance right up to the planned life of the lamp, rather than slowly deteriorate over the whole period.

Left: The two most popular 'colours' of fluorescent tube for marine aquariums are white and actinic blue. The first simulates daylight, the second night-time. Each one will need its own starter gear in the hood, which means that they can be controlled independently. Actinic light is often used to simulate dusk on the reef, when nocturnal fishes, such as cardinalfishes, become more active.

Setting up the lights

The fluorescent tube is retained in the hood by two clips, and held clear of the cover glass. A 75cm (30in) tube has been fitted here, although a 90cm (36in) one would fit.

Fluorescent lighting is relatively economical to run, and replacement tubes are not too expensive. Renew them regularly.

The collecting cup of the protein skimmer is easily accessible behind the aquarium hood.

The front hinged half of the reflector lid is opened for feeding and general maintenance tasks.

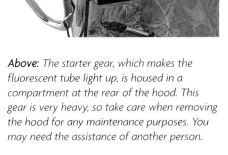

Above: The starter gear, which makes the fluorescent tube light up, is housed in a compartment at the rear of the hood. This gear is very heavy, so take care when removing the hood for any maintenance purposes. You may need the assistance of another person.

Although you may be excited at having – apparently – reached the final stage of the setting-up operation, there is a little further to go before you can safely and successfully introduce fishes into the aquarium. Although the next stage demands very little effort on your part, you may find it difficult to overcome your feelings of impatience as you wait for the aquarium to mature.

It is important that this maturing process is allowed to run its full course, so that the bacteria bed within the filtration system becomes sufficiently established to cope with the waste products that will be generated with the arrival of the fish. It is well worth taking time to understand this process fully, as the whole success of your aquarium depends on it.

The nitrogen cycle

The moment any living organism takes up residence in the aquarium, the business of dealing with waste products becomes a matter of some urgency. Generally speaking, the decomposition of waste products not only uses up vital oxygen, but also produces toxins. The filtration unit installed in our system operates on a multi-method basis: detritus is mechanically strained out of the water by foam in the canister filter, with some dissolved waste elements being adsorbed by any activated carbon medium present. Eventually, colonies of nitrifying bacteria develop within the well-established filter. Two groups of bacteria, *Nitrosomonas* and *Nitrobacter*, consecutively break down ammonia-based waste products, firstly into less toxic nitrite and then into almost harmless nitrate.

How your aquarium matures

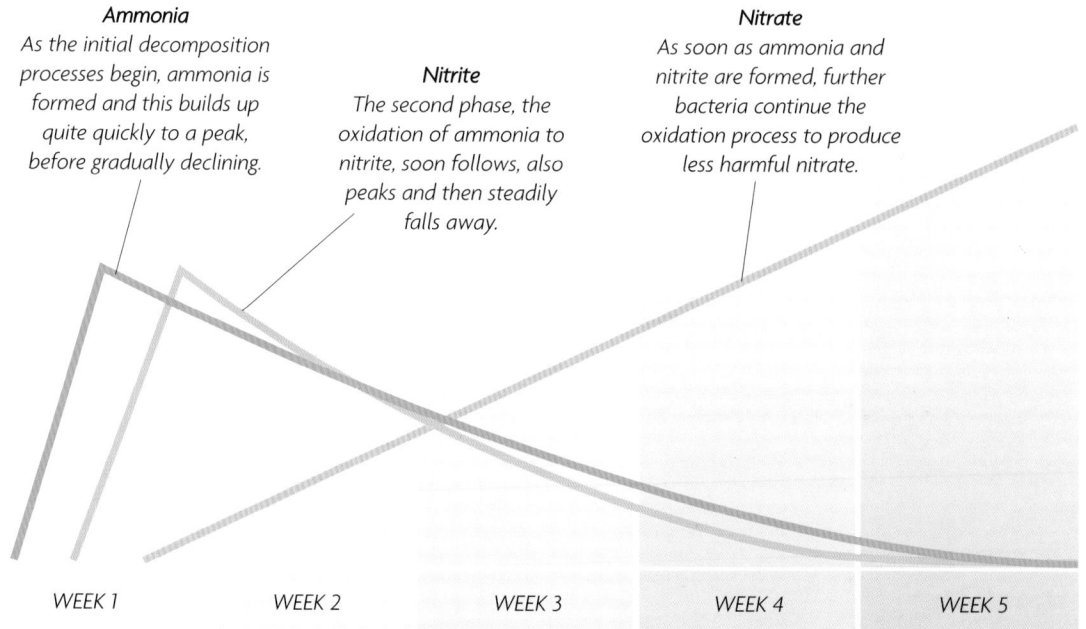

Ammonia
As the initial decomposition processes begin, ammonia is formed and this builds up quite quickly to a peak, before gradually declining.

Nitrite
The second phase, the oxidation of ammonia to nitrite, soon follows, also peaks and then steadily falls away.

Nitrate
As soon as ammonia and nitrite are formed, further bacteria continue the oxidation process to produce less harmful nitrate.

WEEK 1   WEEK 2   WEEK 3   WEEK 4   WEEK 5

The problem for the impatient fishkeeper, itching to introduce the first fishes and complete the tank, is that the maturation process takes time, often up to several months. Using nitrite and nitrate test kits, you can monitor the progress as it occurs. Initially, a 'peak' of ammonia is followed by a rapid build-up of nitrite, which falls dramatically after two or three weeks. Then a slow, steady build-up of nitrate will show in the test results. (Don't worry; this can be controlled by partial water changes.) Only when the nitrite level has fallen to a consistently low level (ideally zero) is it safe to introduce fish into the tank.

Maturing the tank

Operate the tank for at least a week to allow the filter media to become established.

During this period, check that all the equipment is functioning properly and carry out several nitrite and nitrate tests.

Speeding up the maturation

There are two popular methods of speeding up the maturation process. The first is to introduce one or two hardy, inexpensive, nitrite-tolerant fish to produce the necessary 'food' for the bacteria colony to feed upon. The second way is to 'seed' the external filter with a commercially available culture of ready-grown bacteria. Alternatively, when installing the filter, don't use all brand new filter medium; include some 'dirty' medium complete with flourishing bacteria from an established filter unit.

Now you can begin to understand why it is important not to introduce the maximum fish-holding capacity of the tank right from the start. You must give the filtration system enough time to develop. Only by adding livestock at a steady rate over a reasonable period of time can you avoid the onset of 'new tank syndrome', where everything suddenly dies through a filtration overload.

A marine background

Fitting a pictorial background to the aquarium makes the underwater scene look more natural and will hide wallpaper and filter equipment connecting pipes. Secure it with clear adhesive tape (see also page 36).

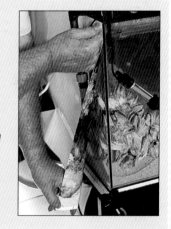

How the nitrogen cycle works

Testing the water involves adding chemicals to a measured sample and comparing the colour change to a printed chart. Some tests involve adding two or three chemicals in stages. Allow the correct time period to elapse between adding reagents. Wear protective gloves when using chemicals, as they may cause skin irritation.

The initial raw material that kicks off the nitrogen cycle is protein-rich food.

Nitrate levels can be controlled by regular partial water changes or by macro-algae using them as 'food'.

Testing for ammonia

0

0.25

0.5

1.0

2.5

5.0

Above: *When testing for ammonia, the aim is to achieve a reading of zero. Not until this reading is consistently at the lowest possible value, is it safe to introduce any fish into the aquarium. Test the water regularly.*

THE NITROGEN CYCLE
The nitrogen cycle is a term applied to the continuous process of the generation and disposal of nitrogenous compounds within the aquarium. The initial wastes are toxic, but are sequentially made safer until they are eventually eliminated from the cycle.

AMMONIA

As ammonia is the first (and most toxic) compound to be produced, it is important to test for it, especially when the aquarium is first set up.

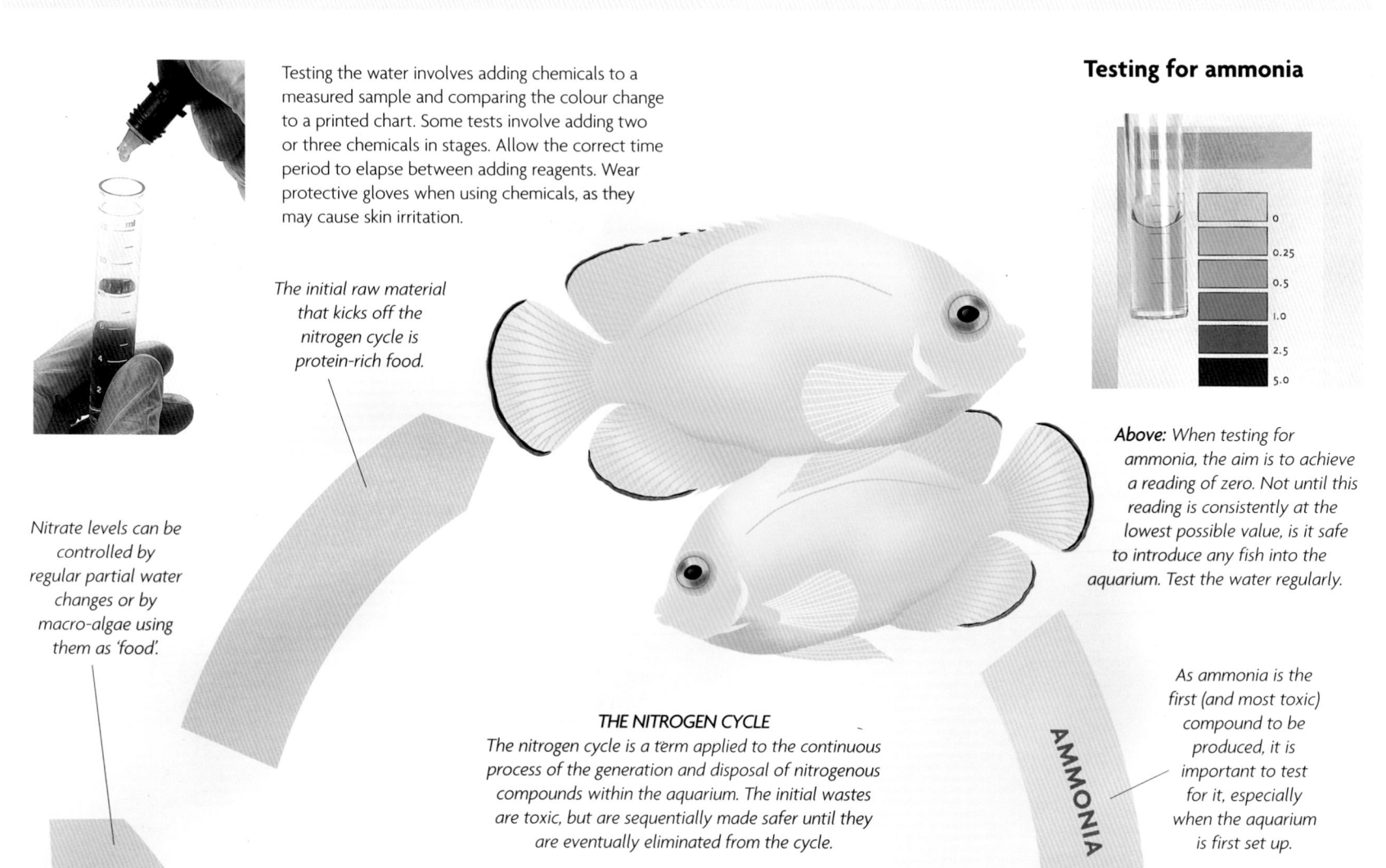

SUBSTRATE AND FILTER MEDIA
The grains of material in the top layer of substrate, the media of a well-established external filter and surfaces in the aquarium, such as rocks and other decorations, are all areas for potential nitrifying bacterial activity.

NITRATE

NITRITE

Nitrobacter *bacteria* continue the nitrification process, converting nitrites to nitrate, a much less toxic compound.

In the second stage of nitrification, ammonia is further converted to less toxic nitrite by Nitrosomas *bacteria*.

Testing for nitrates

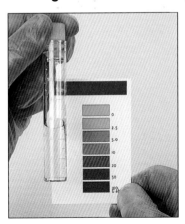

Left: With some original nitrate already present in the mixing water, readings are likely to be high. Although nitrate can be tolerated by some species, it should not be allowed to exceed 10mg/litre. Here, the reading is very low.

Testing for nitrites

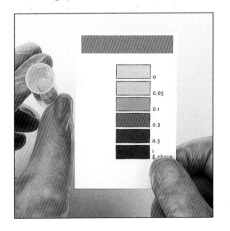

Left: Any indication of the presence of nitrite does at least mean that the bacteria are doing their job in the conversion process but, like ammonia, nitrite is still very toxic and a zero reading is what you need.

STAGE 12 Adding the fish

There may be one or two final touches to be made before the aquarium is finally fully set up and awaiting the first fishes.

Without the presence of bushy plants to act as 'space-fillers' as you would find in a freshwater aquarium, the fully furnished marine aquarium may look rather spartan and austere. Gaping spaces may be visible between the rocky aquarium decorations. These will become increasingly irritating when you realise that the colour of the wall (or the wallpaper) behind the aquarium will be permanently on view through the free-standing aquarium. Of course, this problem will not be quite as noticeable if you house the aquarium within a cabinet, especially if the cabinet has a black wood finish.

To make the aquarium seem part of a larger underwater scene, the rear outside surface of the aquarium – and each end surface if you wish – can be painted a deep blue or, as here, covered with a photographic background of a coral reef scene. Be sure to stretch the background tight against the glass and check that all cables and pipework to and from any equipment are behind the background and not in front of it. Another advantage of a wraparound background is that it will stop unwanted light entering the aquarium from the back and sides, thus preventing green algae from growing on these panels and ensuring that the aquarium is only lit as the coral reef is in nature – from the top.

Earlier in the sequence, you will have fixed a liquid crystal thermometer to the front of the aquarium glass so that you can quickly check on the water temperature. Internal floating, or glass-fixing,

thermometers are also available but most are driven around the tank by water currents and lodge behind a rock, where reading them is just not possible! Where you are using heaters with a temperature-set indicator built into them, align these so that you can see them in case you need to know what temperature they were originally set at.

Make sure that the water level is just above any dark trim fixed to the front top margin of the aquarium; any visible waterline will look unnatural and only reminds you that the tank needs topping up. A final touch might be to touch up the front edge of the polystyrene (or plastic foam) sheet

under the tank with a black permanent spirit marker pen to disguise its otherwise stark whiteness.

With everything now fixed in its final position, the aquarium should be operated as normal. Switch the lights on and off according to the normal daily routine. Leave pumps, filters and airstones running 24 hours a day and allow the aquarium to settle down for a week or two.

Now is the time to consider what fish you want to place in the tank. Having decided on suitable species (see pages 62-73 for suggestions), it is time to buy healthy fish of your choice and bring them home to their new quarters.

Introducing the fish

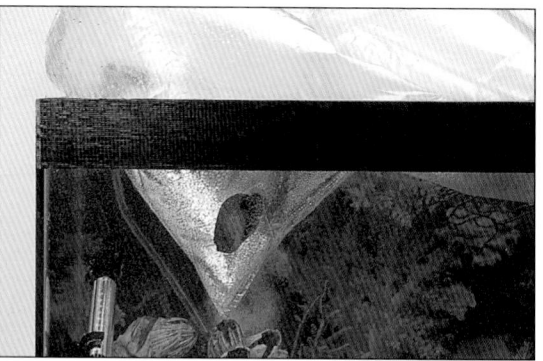

1 To avoid the risk of thermal shock, equalise the temperatures of the water in the tank and in the plastic bag holding the fish, by floating the bags in the tank for 15-20 minutes. Turn off the tank lights to reduce stress.

2 Open the bag and allow the fish to swim out into the aquarium in their own time. Following the introduction of the first fish, quarantine any new livestock in a separate aquarium before adding it to the existing collection.

The finished display

The airstones added to assist salt mixing can be removed if you wish, but the rising bubbles add a pleasing effect to the completed aquarium.

Do not be too impatient to add more fish to the new aquarium. Even with the minimum number of fish, it will take some time to become fully established.

Do not be surprised if your new fish immediately hide behind the decorations. They will come out when they are ready – or hungry!

Healthy fish, such as these clownfishes, require a well-maintained aquarium to thrive.

Part Two:

Options and continuing care

The first part of this guide described the setting up of a basic marine aquarium but, human nature being what it is, there is always room for improvement and experimentation. In all areas, there is basic and sophisticated equipment and in this section of the guide you will find information both on upgrading your system as well as guidance on marine aquarium management, feeding and health care.

Upgrading is not always necessary. Unless you feel your existing system is breaking down and obviously needs replacing, you should stick with your proven successful routines. However, it may be that your fishkeeping ambitions have expanded beyond the basics and you are ready to move on to the new challenges of more delicate fishes and, perhaps, the inclusion of invertebrate life in your aquarium. You may just want to give your existing fishes a better home – in a bigger tank, say – and would like to take advantage of the opportunity to fit newer equipment at the same time.

Aquarium technology is constantly progressing, finding new ways of doing the same essential tasks. For instance, moving most of the hardware out of the tank will result in a less cluttered appearance – and less work trying to disguise (or maintain) the equipment! By 'compartmentalising' each water treatment process, each can be given individual attention, and by 'tuning up' each area you can ensure that your aquarium conditions will be the best possible, rather than trust to one or two units to do their average performance on a compromise basis.

There is an enormous amount of apparently 'must have' equipment available, culminating in completely automatic systems that do everything except wheel your armchair up to the front glass for you. While it is extremely pleasurable to be able to indulge yourself in the very best money can buy, the most important contribution you can make towards the continued well-being of your fishes' is to understand their needs and the workings of the equipment you own to provide it for them. Make use of every technological advance wherever possible but don't become a slave to aquatic fashion; a tank of healthy fish is the ultimate aim, not all the wonderful life-support system surrounding it.

Alternative lighting systems

Our basic aquarium setup is functional and life-supporting as far as the fishes are concerned. However, it does have a 'minimal' appearance that is perhaps not quite what you expected, especially if you are accustomed to the 'busier' underwater scenes at your aquatic store. The lighting system is only sufficient to view the fish; if you want to include other marine life forms, you will need to add some 'life-stimulating' light.

The underwater picture in nature is not limited just to substrate, rocks and fishes. There are living corals, macro-algae and a myriad of invertebrate life forms to complement the scene. It is therefore understandable that as an enthusiastic marine fishkeeper you would want to reflect this fact within the confines of your aquarium, bearing in mind, of course, that you choose compatible species in the first place. However, it is not just a case of buying extra livestock; these are not just decorations, but living organisms, and you must consider their requirements as carefully as those of the fishes.

More light

Many of these organisms are very light-dependent, much more so than the aquarium fish. For instance, many corals may have symbiotic algae growing within them and these simple plant cells require energy in the form of light to live and function normally. Another consideration is that life forms such as corals are not necessarily able to find light by moving towards it. It is important, therefore, that the available light is bright enough to penetrate to the bottom of the aquarium where sedentary

invertebrates may be based. This in turn necessitates the clarity of the water being maintained at all times if the invertebrates are not to be denied their life-giving energy.

When considering keeping invertebrate life it is usual to maximise existing light levels or to add additional lighting to that already present in the system. The first strategy to put into action is adding 'clip-on' reflectors to the fluorescent tubes so that all the generated light is reflected down into the water rather than some of it spilling upwards into

Right: The brilliant tropical sun, blazing down on the coral reef, stimulates and sustains the growth of fishes and invertebrates alike, but need only be replicated in the aquarium if a complete underwater scene is to be created. Such high lighting levels are not required for a 'fish-only' collection.

the hood. Secondly, adding extra fluorescent tubes in the hood will certainly increase the light levels.

You may consider converting the system to a pendant lighting system, in which case the hood is discarded and the cover glass is the only 'top' to the aquarium. The extra lighting will probably result in more growth of algae, which will benefit any herbivorous fish present in the aquarium. To take further advantage of the increased light energy, you could consider keeping various forms of *Caulerpa*, the macro-algae. Suddenly switching over from one lighting system to another can cause stress to the fish as well as upset the biological balance in the aquarium, with algal blooms occurring. Equally important is the effect of the higher powered (and thus hotter) lights on water temperatures; make sure the lamps are well-ventilated to disperse any generated heat.

Another feature of some invertebrate life is the presence of fluorescing cells in their structure. By utilising an actinic fluorescent tube you can not only cause the cells to glow after the rest of the aquarium lighting has been switched off, but also provide a moonlight effect for the benefit of the more nocturnally active inhabitants.

Below: *This hanging pendant lighting system is designed to hang over the water surface; no hood is required but a cover glass should still be used to prevent splash damage to the lights.*

Left: *The provision of white and blue fluorescent in combination with a metal halide lamp offers the fishkeeper the facility of creating separate day and night lighting effects, together with a 'hot' highlighted area to feature specially chosen decor or invertebrate life in the tank.*

In this model the tube fits through plastic formers that clip into a flexible reflective sheet to create the shape.

This pendant fitting reduces glare into the room and can be positioned exactly over the aquarium.

Above: *Fitting an enhancing reflector means that all the light from the fluorescent tube is directed downwards into the aquarium.*

Alternative filtration systems

In our setup tank, an external power filter extracts water from the aquarium, mechanically filters it and then returns the water to the aquarium. This reduces the amount of debris suspended in the water, keeping the water clear, maximises the amount of light reaching the bottom of the aquarium, and assists in gaseous exchanges at the water surface by creating turbulence. An external power filter can also be used as a pre-filter to remove debris from water being delivered to any supplementary filtration equipment (see below).

Filtration options
Extra filtration units, in addition to the already-installed system, can produce extra water clarity and can also provide beneficial water currents throughout the aquarium.

Internal power filter units can be installed at various points around the aquarium and even connected to a time switch system so as to simulate tidal flows. One provision if you are using such systems in a reef tank is that they may need to be switched off while you are feeding the invertebrate life in the aquarium, as their powerful action will remove the food from the water before the invertebrate life can make use of it.

Additional extra components to the filtration system include those using activated carbon to adsorb dissolved matter, those that remove phosphates, denitrification units, simple sponge filters (ideal for quarantine and treatment tanks) and 'Kalkwasser' units that add calcium to the water. Kalkwasser, also referred to as limewater, is produced by passing carbon dioxide through calcium oxide in water. This can be achieved by using a unit built into the filtration system in the sump, although Kalkwasser can be added separately rather than automatically if preferred; a common practice is to use it when topping-up evaporation losses.

Above: Simulate tidal flows in the aquarium by installing powerheads around the tank. Position them at the surface and at varying levels in the water; remember to guard their intakes. This powerhead is fitted with an air intake to inject extra aeration at, or near, the water surface.

Internal filter

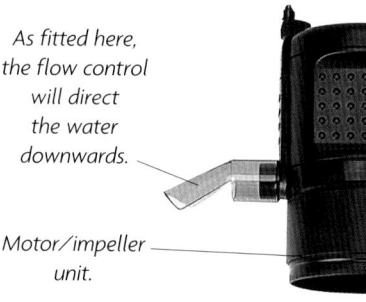

As fitted here, the flow control will direct the water downwards.

Motor/impeller unit.

Chamber for activated carbon.

Foam insert slides into filter canister.

Right: The components of the filter push-fit together. Read the instructions carefully to ensure that everything lines up and never use force. Small filters are useful in quarantine and treatment tanks, but take up swimming space in the main aquarium.

Fluidised bed filter system

Fluidised bed units take biological filtration out of the tank and supersede outdated substrate systems. Silica sand is held in suspension in aquarium water pumped through an external cylindrical container. Because the sand granules are free to move, and not packed together, they offer a much larger surface area for bacterial colonisation and this results in a much more efficient nitrification process.

In some models, an incorporated carbon filter cartridge removes any coloration from the water before it returns to the aquarium. The fluidised bed system is oxygen-consuming and water emerging from such units should be given every chance to re-oxygenate before returning to the main aquarium. This may be achieved by using a spraybar as a return tube, a venturi system fitted to the outlet or even an airstone placed at the point of the returning water.

Some thought should also be given as to what happens should the electricity supply be cut off or debris block the inlet of the fluidised bed unit. (Some form of pre-filtering will prevent the latter occurring). Obviously, the water flow through the unit will stop but, more importantly, the 'filter bed' will physically collapse from its previous 'in suspension' form to a solid mass of sand. On the resumption of power, the pump may not have enough energy to 're-suspend' the sand without a little help, with consequent damage to the pump. (If possible, adjust the flow to maximum on restarting, and then reset it to normal flow rate.) Equally problematical for the aquarium would be the rapid demise of the bacterial colony should the power failure last an appreciable length of time. When restarting after a lengthy period, run the unit in a monitored 'closed system' situation until tests show the bacterial bed has become re-established.

A fluidised bed filter

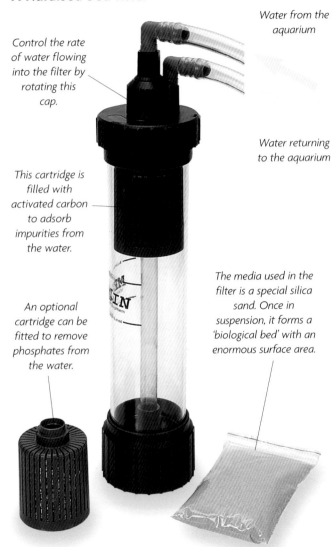

Control the rate of water flowing into the filter by rotating this cap.

Water from the aquarium

Water returning to the aquarium

This cartridge is filled with activated carbon to adsorb impurities from the water.

An optional cartridge can be fitted to remove phosphates from the water.

The media used in the filter is a special silica sand. Once in suspension, it forms a 'biological bed' with an enormous surface area.

Above: *When in operation, the sand's moving biological bed is held in suspension (the two lines show the upper and lower levels of the medium). A valve in the unit prevents sand siphoning back into the pump if the power fails.*

Alternative filtration systems

Ultraviolet light (UV) sterilisers

Another method of keeping the aquarium 'clean' incorporates the use of ultraviolet light. As the aquarium water passes close to the UV light, waterborne organisms (good as well as bad) are killed by the UV rays. Efficiency is proportional to 'exposure' time: longest is best. Renew the lamp every six months for best results. Its application is usually limited to commercial aquatic stores operating a central filtration system. UV light is not just another 'colour' of fluorescent tube. Never use UV light as a source of illumination and never where the tube can be seen by the naked eye.

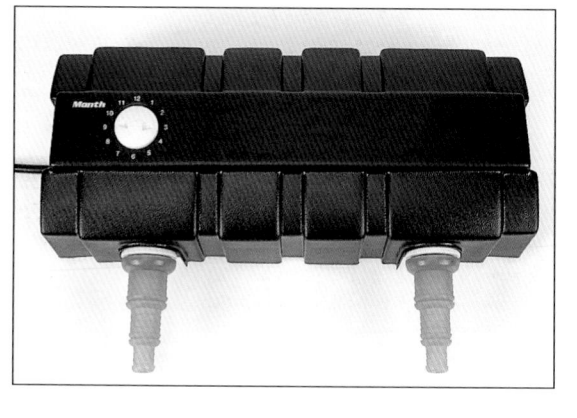

Above: *The aquarium water can be sterilised by passing it through a UV unit. The water hose connectors are translucent so that you can see the 'glow' of the UV lamp when in operation, a safety measure to make sure you don't open the unit and damage your eyesight.*

Using live rock in the aquarium

While we have configured our basic aquarium with a protein skimmer and an external filter, the 'biological' purification of the water can also be achieved by using another natural method making use of 'live rock'. This is simply rock collected from the wild with living organisms already in situ. The base material is usually of a labyrinthine, highly-porous nature and provides both aerobic and anaerobic areas inhabited by the various minute animals and bacteria. These actively purify the water in much the same way as the bacteria in our external filter. This system has become known as the 'Berlin method'.

In the Berlin method, more reliance is placed upon 'live rock' and protein skimming in the aquarium to rid it effectively of unwanted toxic materials. The theory is that the protein skimmer removes organic matter before it degenerates into ammonia and therefore obviates the need for its subsequent conversion to nitrite and nitrate by bacteria; the inclusion of large areas of live rock also reduces the load on biological filtration systems. One drawback of using live rock is that it is expensive and furnishing the aquarium with a suitable amount may prove to be a financial deterrent to many fishkeepers.

Live rock is maintained at the aquatic store and may even be inoculated with new living cultures during this time. Obviously, taking the usual pre-cleaning precautions as described for ordinary 'decorative' rocks would not apply in this instance. It is vital that live rocks are introduced into oxygenated water as soon as possible; depending on their quality (a known history is highly preferable) you may put them into your main collection immediately, although treating them to a quarantine period (as you would with any new additional livestock) could be a prudent measure. During quarantine, it may be likely that some organisms will die off and new ones re-emerge; fluctuations in nitrite and nitrate levels will occur and the conditions should be left to stabilise before transferring the rocks to their new permanent home.

Unless the aquarium is to be set up with live rock from the outset, only small amounts should be introduced into an established system at a time to avoid fluctuations in redox potential.

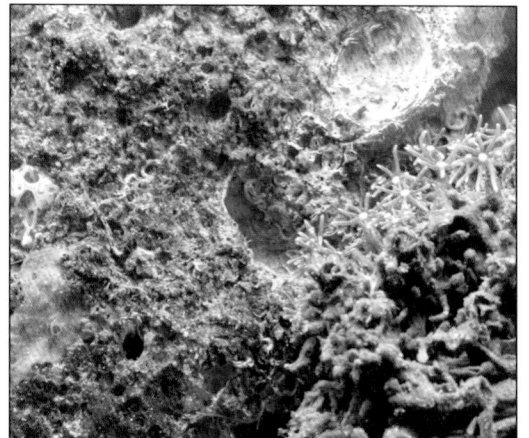

Using ozone in the aquarium

In the quest for ever-increasing hygiene in the aquarium, the use of ozone (O_3) has often been practised, usually in association with protein skimming, where its highly dangerous oxidising qualities are kept within the protein skimmer chamber and thus safely separated from the livestock in the aquarium. (Ozone is a highly unstable form of oxygen with three oxygen atoms. It breaks down rapidly and the extra oxygen atom oxidises toxins and kills bacteria and other microorganisms in the water.) While ozone undoubtedly has its uses, it needs careful handling and is best left to the more experienced fishkeeper. Automatic control of ozone levels is possible using a redox probe in association with the ozone generator.

Redox is a contraction of the words 'reduction' and 'oxidation' and the redox potential (measured in millivolts) might be regarded as an indication of the well-being of the aquarium, as the reduction and oxidation processes are two of the most vital in the 'metabolism' of aquarium conditions. There can be no hard and fast ideal value (it is always changing); levels found in nature are usually in the range 200-400mV, with those in the aquarium slightly lower.

With the constantly varying conditions in the aquarium, any 'test kit' result is only worth its value at the time of testing: it is the changes and/or rapidity of these changes that indicate problems. Learn to interpret the readings and their fluctuations before jumping to conclusions: observe the fish – if they are healthy and acting normally, don't meddle with things!

Ozone and protein skimming

Above: *Activated carbon placed in a compartment on top of the collecting cup prevents any excess ozone entering the atmosphere.*

Froth carrying organic waste overflows into this collecting cup.

The waste can be drained from the base of the collecting cup through this tube.

The ozone generator uses a high-energy electrical discharge to bond an extra atom to oxygen molecules to create ozone (O_3)

A check valve prevents water siphoning back into the ozoniser. Renew regularly.

Ozone passes into the water flow through the venturi device located here.

This probe hangs in the aquarium. It measures the redox potential of the water and regulates the amount of ozone produced by the ozoniser.

Alternative filtration systems

The Jaubert system

Until relatively recently, marine aquariums relied on mechanical, chemical and biological methods of filtration using long-established conventional units. One innovative progression in the 1980s was the Jaubert system, best described as a subgravel system without any uplift tube or any deliberately engineered water flow through it. Primarily designed for use in Dr Jaubert's own Monaco Oceanographic Aquarium, this system's basics soon attracted interest and several American marine fishkeepers, such as Bob Goemans, adapted it with some success for use in the more modest-sized home aquarium. Details are included here for reference.

A plastic grid (fluorescent light diffusing grids are ideal) is held off the bottom of the tank by plastic supports to create a static void (plenum). A thin layer of synthetic floss material covers the grid to prevent material trickling downwards and the rest of the substrate placed over it. The natural diffusion of oxygen downwards from the main, additionally-aerated body of water towards the oxygen-depleted plenum sustains the biological filtration action within the substrate, whilst bacteria in the anaerobic plenum act as denitrifiers, reducing nitrate levels and completing the full nitrogen cycle.

The quality of the original mixing water

The difference between an 'easy' and a 'delicate' fish could be their respective reactions to water composition. Get to recognise such species and also learn what they need in water preparation terms. For the 'fish-only' collection we have featured in this

The Jaubert system

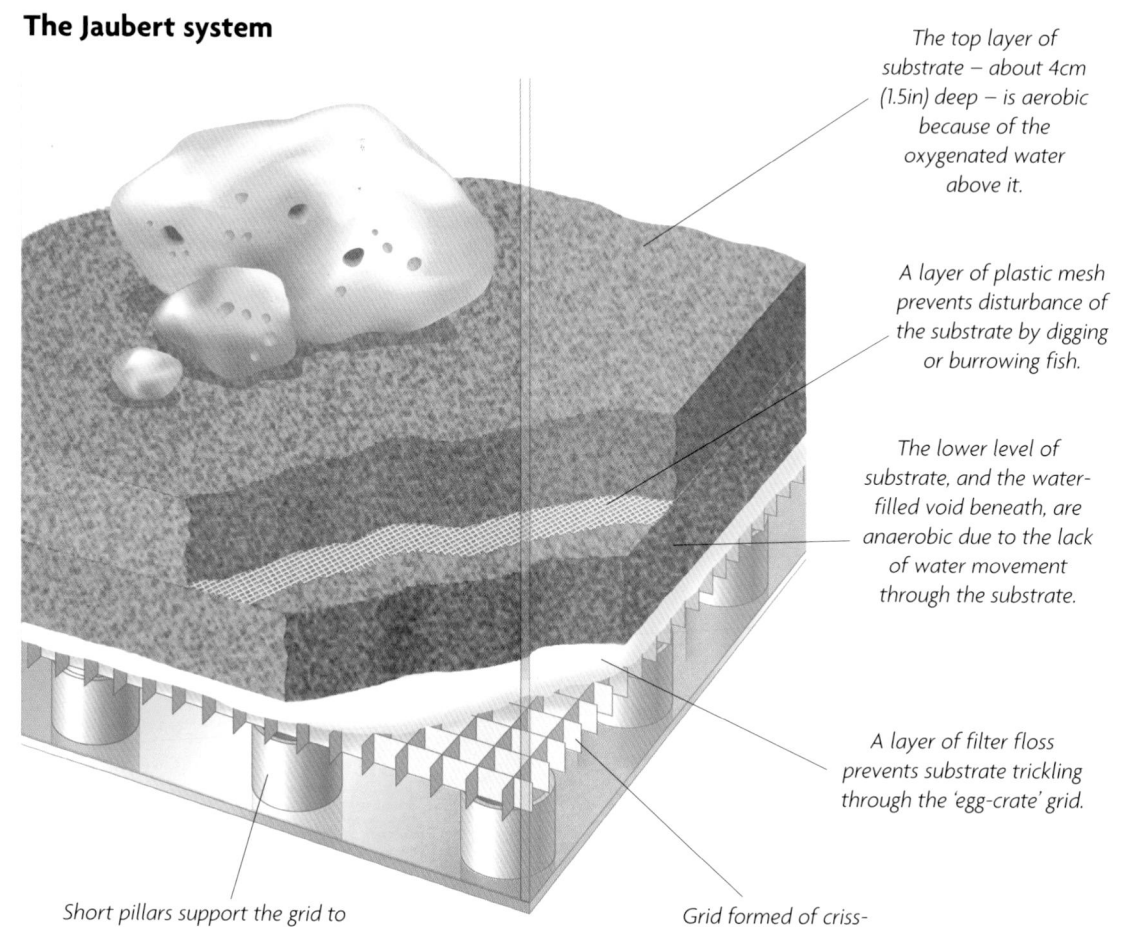

The top layer of substrate – about 4cm (1.5in) deep – is aerobic because of the oxygenated water above it.

A layer of plastic mesh prevents disturbance of the substrate by digging or burrowing fish.

The lower level of substrate, and the water-filled void beneath, are anaerobic due to the lack of water movement through the substrate.

A layer of filter floss prevents substrate trickling through the 'egg-crate' grid.

Short pillars support the grid to create a void about 2.5cm (1in) deep beneath the substrate.

Grid formed of criss-crossed plastic slats.

guide, over-zealous attention to water preparation may not be actually as necessary as it would be for more delicate species of fish and for reef-type tanks that include invertebrate life.

Whilst the manufacturers of the salt mixes do all they can to provide reliable, high-quality raw materials, they cannot be held responsible for the quality of waters used in the mixing processes. It should be appreciated that fishkeeping is not high on the list of considerations of companies providing domestic water supplies: their duty is to provide water suitable for human consumption, which means the addition of certain disinfecting agents, notably chlorine and chloramine. Providing that the preparation of seawater is carried out at least 24-48 hours before its use (some authorities recommend a week's duration) and constant aeration and correct heating applied, then the majority of fishes within basic fish-only collections should not be at risk.

Where the inhabitants of the marine aquarium are to be more delicate species, and especially where invertebrates are to be included too, the original 'mixing water' may require prior treatment before use to remove harmful substances such as heavy metals and to remove or neutralise the previously mentioned disinfecting agents.

A popular (albeit sometimes expensive) method of achieving purer water is by means of the reverse osmosis (R.O.) process. Forcing water through a semi-permeable membrane will result in the unwanted substances being left

Right: For the chance to see anemonefishes happy in the embrace of sea anemone tentacles, you must provide the best possible water quality in the tank. Invertebrate life is usually the first to suffer when bad conditions prevail.

Left: Tapwater can contain contaminants. These can be removed using a reverse osmosis unit such as this. The efficiency of such units depends on the concentration of pollutants present in the water supply. Make sure you buy the correct unit for your usage.

behind, with only pure water emerging from the R.O. unit. The expense incurred using this method is in the quantity of waste water produced for each amount of usable water; of course, this amount depends on just how 'contaminated' the original water was at the outset and this will vary from area to area and from supplier to supplier.

Alternatively, you can produce 'purer' water from the domestic supply by using deionising resins, although it is vital that you understand how these resins work before you use them. Again, the process can be costly and wasteful in areas of highly contaminated domestic water supplies.

Alternative filtration systems

Reef tanks

For the marine fishkeeper who wants everything provided, the reef aquarium must be the ultimate answer. The tank comes ready engineered, fitted with filtration systems, heating and lighting and it is almost just a case of fitting a power plug, filling it with water and everything is ready to go.

As an alternative to the 'complete system', the modular concept has the filtration system fitted beneath the main aquarium within a high-quality cabinet. Water enters the system by means of an overflowing weir from the main aquarium and the whole filtration unit will probably employ nitrification towers, wet-and-dry sections and, in some cases, denitrification units as well. Filtered water is usually held in a sump (the aquarium heater could be placed here, too) before being pumped back to the main display aquarium.

One problem with all marine aquariums housed in cabinets is the damage that can be caused by salt-laden condensation, which can lead to veneers lifting and serious staining occurring.

Right: It would be hard to tell at first glance whether you are seeing a part of a real natural coral reef or not, such is the excellence of this superbly maintained reef tank display.

Down in the sump

The sump beneath a reef aquarium is a 'high-tech' environment full of tubes and boxes that maintain the water conditions in the display tank above it. Here is a quick rundown of what's going on down there.

Water reaches the sump by overflowing from the main aquarium and, once cleaned, is returned by a pump situated in the sump. In the 'wet-and-dry' filter, the incoming aquarium water is fed over a mass of plastic balls on its way to the other water treatment components. Being in the atmosphere rather than totally submerged, the nitrifying bacteria that flourish here are well provided with oxygen and so operate more efficiently.

The calcium reactor is filled with calcium oxide and the water passing through it (also enriched with carbon dioxide) carries added calcium back to the aquarium.

Nitrates can be removed by means of a denitrator unit in which bacteria live in anaerobic conditions. As they 'feed' they take their necessary oxygen from the nitrates, thus reducing them back to nitrogen gas.

In-sump systems can also accommodate protein skimmers, phosphate removers, freshwater 'topping up' reservoirs and even the heating system, thus de-cluttering the main viewing area of the aquarium and giving the fish more swimming room, too.

Right: A reef tank offers a home to invertebrate life as well as fishes. Although colourful soft corals provide a backdrop, extra interest is provided by the activities of more mobile species such as this elegant painted shrimp, Lysmata amboinensis.

Above: Where the aquarium is housed in a cabinet, it makes good sense to have the water treatment equipment assembled in one convenient place - out of sight but easily accessible for maintenance tasks.

Feeding marine fish

Ideally, the best diet for any animals in captivity should be based on the food they would have enjoyed in nature, so we should not be surprised that the best diet for the majority of marine fishes is fish! The exceptions to this general rule are fish that are herbivorous by nature or those whose tiny mouths mean that they feed on microscopic animals such as plankton.

The shape of a fish's head or snout is a good clue as to how it obtains its food. For example, butterflyfishes often have elongated snouts, ideally suited to picking food from crevices within the coral reef. Parrotfishes have strong fused teeth with which they crunch up the coral in search of food. The fearsome jaws of groupers and lionfish are obviously

Right: Frozen foods are sold in single slabs (simply break off pieces as required) or in individual push-out 'servings'. Thaw frozen foods before use to prevent fish eating ice.

Frozen foods

Whole cockle
This natural food is accepted by all marine fishes.

Marine mix
This is a mixture of various natural marine invertebrate and fish meats.

Krill
A nutritious food for larger fish; break up for small fishes.

Fish
These small fish make excellent 'one-gulp' food for larger fishes.

Shrimp
Many wild-caught foods are irradiated to destroy disease pathogens.

designed for copious food-gathering. The mouths of blennies and gobies are located at the very front of the head and the flat ventral surface of the body brings the mouth into efficient proximity with the food-laden substrate.

A feeding regime

Other considerations are when – and how often – to feed fish, and here again, observing nature will help the fishkeeper. Large-mouthed, predatory fish may gorge themselves initially and then fast for a few hours; herbivorous grazers appear to be active as long as there is daylight. However, the majority of fishes in the aquarium will be satisfied with one or two regular feeds each day. Do not neglect the needs of the more nocturnal species. They should be fed after the aquarium lights have been switched off for a little while.

On balance, the fishkeeper would be well-advised to underfeed, rather than to give food every time the fish appear to indicate that they require it by their behaviour at the front glass. You will know if you are

Flakes and granules

Flake foods fall slowly through the water and are ideal for most midwater and upper water level species.

Mixed flakes

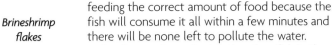

Brineshrimp flakes

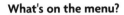

Granular food
This sinks quickly for the benefit of bottom-dwellers.

Freeze-dried foods

Based on fresh natural foods, most freeze-dried portions can be stuck onto the interior glass panels at any level.

Freeze-dried river shrimp

feeding the correct amount of food because the fish will consume it all within a few minutes and there will be none left to pollute the water.

Feeding marine animals other than fish in the aquarium may require special techniques. For example, in the case of filter-feeding invertebrates in a reef tank, it may be best to turn off the filtration system briefly, so that the action of the filter does not remove the food from the aquarium before the invertebrates can make use of it.

What's on the menu?

All suitable foods for marine aquarium fishes should be processed in one form or another. Unless the source is meticulously screened, providing live food

Tablet food
Excellent for sticking on the tank glass.

Freeze-dried krill

Freeze-dried brineshrimp

Above: *This decorated dartfish (Nemateleotris decora) is a midwater feeder and obviously has no problems in capturing food as it falls through the water. Here, it is about to 'capture' a fragment of thawed-out shrimp.*

runs the risk of introducing undesirable pathogens to the aquarium. There is a school of thought that believes that offering live fish, such as goldfish, to the larger, more predatory marine fish in the aquarium may lead to the marines 'learning' to be predatory towards their smaller tankmates.

Given that the ideal diet should be marine-based, you will find all manner of frozen fish- and shellfish-based foods available at your local aquatic retailer. It is likely that these will have been processed using gamma irradiation to safeguard against the introduction of disease. The freeze-drying process may also be employed to preserve aquatic animals as prospective food, and such products are also readily available.

Much research has been done by the fish food manufacturers and a whole range of recipes suitable for marine fish will be available in many forms: flake food, tablets, granules or even sticks. While such foods may appear expensive, it is false economy to

Feeding marine fish

buy a large amount, especially if you only have one aquarium. Once the food container has been opened, the quality of the food (and the important vitamin content) will gradually deteriorate, thus denying your fish all the benefits the manufacturers have engineered into the food.

Feeding herbivorous marine fish

Dealing with the needs of herbivorous species is not as difficult as you might imagine. If the lighting level is sufficiently strong, a healthy growth of algae should soon manifest itself over the surface of the aquarium walls and decorations, and herbivorous species will be only too glad to graze on this green matter. Alternatively, culture algae-covered rocks in a separate tank standing in a sunny position and filled

Right: Presenting non-aquatic green foods to marine fish is not difficult. These lettuce leaves are weighted down on the substrate between two halves of a magnetic algae scraper.

Below: Many of the popular species of fish browse on green matter in the aquarium. Caulerpa, a naturally-growing marine macro-algae, can be encouraged to grow under powerful lighting conditions and provide necessary diet material for herbivorous species.

with discarded aquarium water following a water change. Transfer each 'green' rock to the main aquarium in rotation, and replace the 'grazed upon' rocks in the culture tank. This should ensure a steady vegetable diet for those fish that need it.

Provide a further source of vegetable matter in the form of lettuce leaves, spinach and peas. It is worth blanching or lightly bruising the leaves first. Clamp them between the two halves of a magnetic algae scraper to prevent them circulating around the aquarium under the influence of water currents.

Preparing your own fish food

For fishkeepers with more than one aquarium and a larger demand for food, there is always the possibility of preparing your own fish food. Blend together suitable ingredients, such as canned or frozen prawns, cockles, shrimps or spinach, in a gelatin base and freeze them until needed.

However convenient it may be to settle on an easily obtained or conveniently prepared food, it is important to vary the diet as much as possible. This is the only way of ensuring not only that the fish receive all the nutrients they require, but also that they do not become bored with a routine menu and consequently go on hunger strike. Fish that are actively feeding when you buy them are far more likely to recommence regular feeding once they are in your aquarium. Unfortunately, there are occasions when even a fish that is feeding regularly loses weight despite an apparently healthy appetite. In this instance, check the conditions in the aquarium; sometimes, a slightly larger than normal water change may induce a return to normality.

Left: Clearly this clownfish trusts the hand that feeds it and appreciates the food, too. Avoid putting your hands in the tank if they have wounds or abrasions (or wear rubber gloves). Similarly, if there are fish that bite or have venomous fins in the tank then even further caution is advised.

Routine maintenance

At first, you will need to carry out regular tests on various aspects of water quality until you become accustomed to the routine of aquarium maintenance and develop an eye for varying conditions. As all these tests are comparative, be sure to perform checks at the same time of day and under the same conditions, so that each result can be interpreted correctly against those obtained before. In this way, you can see how your aquarium is developing and quickly spot any adverse trends. With all tests, sudden changes are more significant than the actual readings. Always take steps to determine the cause – a dead fish somewhere, inadvertent overfeeding?

Periodic monitoring of the pH level will reveal any deterioration in water quality (a falling pH is the sign to look for). If this happens, carry out a partial water change. It is common practice to carry out a water change of approximately 25% every two to three weeks. As a guide, natural seawater has a pH of between 7.8 and 8.4, depending on location and water depths, but it is usual to find that salt mixes made up with normal tapwater generally return a final reading towards the higher end of the range.

Checks for nitrite and nitrate will reveal occasional 'peaks' as and when you add new livestock, but providing you make these additions gradually, the system should be able to cope.

The specific gravity will also change over a period of time, slightly increasing as freshwater evaporates from the aquarium. Paradoxically, this is the one occasion when you can safely top up the aquarium with fresh, rather than salt, water. Topping up with saltwater will only increase the specific gravity.

A maintenance schedule

Task	Frequency (new tank)	Frequency (old tank)
Check ammonia, nitrite, nitrate.	Every week (up to week 8)	Monthly or when needed
Check pH level.	Every two weeks (up to week 8)	Every six weeks or when needed
Check specific gravity.	Every week (up to week 8)	Monthly; after all water changes and when needed
Partial water change (lightly stocked tank) (heavily stocked tank	Every month Every two weeks	Every month Every two weeks
Empty protein skimmer cup and clean interior of protein skimmer.	As needed	As needed
Clean cover glass/reflector and remove algae. Check airstones.	As needed	As needed
Rinse/replace filter media. Cut filter sponge in half and clean alternately.	Every month	Every month
Top up evaporation losses (with freshwater or Kalkwasser only).	As needed	As needed
Check for dead fish, signs of disease, bullying and abnormal behaviour.	Daily	Daily
Check equipment, temperature and flow rate.	Daily	Daily

Mixing for partial water changes

Regular partial water changes must become permanent fixtures on the 'to do' list if water quality is to be maintained. As it is no longer possible to mix salt in the tank, it is vital that any containers used are reserved exclusively for that purpose. Do not use any handy bucket and certainly no metal buckets at all. After a time, you will be able to judge just how much 'salt per bucketful' makes how many litres of

Testing pH level

Left: Before using reagents, shake the bottle well. When adding reagents to the sample tube, check how many drops are needed and count them accurately. Make sure that each 'drop' is a genuine, complete drop and not half reagent and half air.

Left: It is simple to compare the colour of liquid in the sample tube against the colour card. Make sure you do it properly; not all tests use the same method (even those from the same manufacturer). Some ask you to view the colour down, and not through the tube.

seawater. Make a mental note of the weight of salt used and make a mark (using a spirit pen on the outside of the bucket) to show the appropriate water level in the bucket.

Use an aquarium heater-thermostat to get the water up to temperature before adding any water treatments and salt mix. Always aerate replacement water at least overnight (or longer if possible) before adding it to the tank. Switch off the heater and allow it to cool down before removing it from the bucket, but don't let the water cool too much before using it.

Remember that any discarded water following a water change can be used to hatch brineshrimp, rather than just being disposed of down the drain.

Care of filters

The external filter will require regular maintenance and, providing a pair of isolating taps have been fitted into the hoses, there is no great upheaval needed in order to service the filter unit itself.

If used, carbon will need replacing probably about every six months but the 'floss' type medium can be rinsed through (using some aquarium water, not tapwater) and re-used. Any biological medium in the filter should also be treated with respect; a light rinse with aquarium water while it is still in the filter will flush away any fine particles without adversely

Use non-metallic containers and implements when mixing salt for the aquarium. Keep a plastic bucket exclusively for this purpose.

affecting the bacteria within the medium. At the same time, check that the holes in the spraybar are not blocked. Obviously, the protein skimmer's collecting cup will need regular emptying. Periodically, use a bottlebrush to clean the interior walls to clear them of any accumulated fatty films that would otherwise impair the skimmer's performance.

General tank maintenance

Try not to intrude into the tank too much. Using a long-handled scraper to remove algae from the glass walls is better than putting your hands into the tank. You will soon become accustomed to gauging the water temperature by touching the outside of the tank with the palm of your hand, rather than depending on the thermometer. Airstones soon become blocked in the marine aquarium and should be cleaned (by boiling) or simply renewed.

Care of lighting

Replace fluorescent tubes every six months and keep the cover glass or condensation tray clear of algae and any other dust or dirt that may impede light transfer through it. Similarly, clean reflectors fitted around tubes in the hood and those in pendant-style light fittings; be on the lookout for any salt that may have become deposited.

Basic health care

It could be argued that the best way of dealing with disease is to avoid ever having a breakout in the first place, and there is much to be said in favour of the argument that prevention is better than cure.

By following the steps in this book, you will have set up an aquarium that provides the best living conditions, so don't spoil things by buying fish that may not be fully healthy. It is vital that your fish are in the best condition at the moment they become your responsibility, so always follow the guidelines for selecting good-quality fish (see pages 60-61).

Nevertheless, it is a fact of life that, at some time or another, every fishkeeper will have to face up to an outbreak of disease in the aquarium.

Look and learn

Naturally, as a fishkeeper you will spend much time looking at your fish, but you should get into the habit of learning from what you see. Once you have become used to recognising each fish's normal behaviour, you will soon be able to detect any abnormalities, such as erratic swimming, sulking and hiding away. Concave profiles (especially on a new fish) should be regarded with suspicion.

Do not be influenced by the guideline applied to freshwater fishes that clamped-down fins are indicative of ill health; many marine fish, such as birdmouth wrasse, swim with their fins folded down

Right: This wreckfish (Anthias squamipinnis) *is everything a healthy fish should be. Its colours are bright, with well-defined patterns. The skin is free of spots, wounds or other blemishes, and the body has no sunken in areas.*

as a matter of course, and in any case, some species lack some fins found on other fishes!

First things first

When dealing with disease, you should not only identify the ailment, but also look for signs of what might have caused it. Always check the aquarium conditions (especially water parameters) first. Most ailments in the aquarium are brought about by stress, which is itself triggered by several factors –

overcrowding, poor aquarium conditions and the introduction of new, unquarantined stock. Attention to aquarium hygiene, modest stocking levels and quarantining all new stock will do much to ensure that your aquarium remains stress- and disease-free.

If you have a second aquarium set up as a quarantine tank for any new stock, it can be easily pressed into service as a hospital or treatment tank. If you haven't got such a tank, then now might be a good time to get one!

Being isolated from the wild, the aquarium would appear to be a safe environment. However, captive marine fish can still fall prey to the occasional ailment. Many common problems have easily detectable, external, visible symptoms, such as tiny white spots, etc. These can be treated successfully using commercially available treatments. Internal disorders, with external symptoms that may not become apparent until the disease has progressed too far for successful treatment, are more difficult to deal with and usually result in the loss of the fish concerned. Some remedies are not always available worldwide due to differing regulations on drug sales.

The treatment tank

Using a proprietary remedy in a filtered system may cause problems, and this is where a separate treatment tank comes into its own. Firstly, some medications can affect the nitrifying bacteria, with the result that the main tank needs time to 'remature' once treatment is complete. If this is the case, the fish could be under further stress during this period. A further problem occurs if you are using external or supplementary filters that employ carbon. The treatment will be removed from the aquarium water as it passes through the carbon and be rendered ineffective. For this reason, you should always remove carbon from the filtration system before dosing with treatments.

Copper remedies

Bear in mind that it is not possible to treat fishes in the aquarium if invertebrates are also present. Although fish respond well to copper-based remedies, invertebrates have no tolerance to them at all and will be killed.

If you are treating fish in a separate tank, be sure to return their water conditions to those of the main aquarium before transferring them back, otherwise they will become stressed upon transition and you may find that disease sets in once again.

Tread carefully

Do not go about treating a fish in a haphazard way. Be methodical in your approach and make notes if necessary. You should be confident of your diagnosis before buying one of the highly effective treatments available for treating a variety of common problems. In an emergency, some parasitic attacks can be dealt with by a simple freshwater bath. Although it sounds contradictory, a bath in freshwater for some minutes (less if the fish shows signs of discomfort) can bring relief to marine fish.

It might not be possible to arrive at an accurate diagnosis straightaway, since there may be more than one explanation for any given symptom. For example, fishes with breathing difficulty may not be the subject of a parasitic attack at all; it may be that there is simply not sufficient oxygen in the water available to them. (That is why it is so important to check the water conditions first.) However, if the fish's gills really are covered with parasites, then this will cut down the efficiency with which they can extract oxygen from the water and results in their rapid, gasping breathing actions.

Dosing the tank

Accurate dosing is very important. Do not merely tip the treatment into the aquarium and hope for the best, and most certainly do not add another remedy immediately should the first one not work, as combining several remedies may be toxic. Because recommended dosages are generally related to the

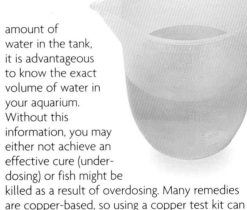

Right: Pre-mix medication in a little tank water before adding it to the treatment tank. This helps rapid dispersion and also stops fish eating the droplets!

amount of water in the tank, it is advantageous to know the exact volume of water in your aquarium. Without this information, you may either not achieve an effective cure (under-dosing) or fish might be killed as a result of overdosing. Many remedies are copper-based, so using a copper test kit can also help to ensure that your dosing is correct. In addition, by monitoring copper levels following treatment, you can also make sure that every bit of the treatment has been removed

Typical curable ailments

Ailments caused by parasitic attack are some of the most common to strike at aquarium fishes. Fortunately, the symptoms of such attacks are easy to spot: tiny spots or an all-over dusting effect may appear on the body, the fish may have a rapid breathing action or may repeatedly scratch or 'flick' itself on a rock or on the substrate.

Basic health care

White spot

As its name suggests, the symptoms are a covering of tiny white spots on the body and fins. Caused by the parasite *Cryptocaryon irritans*, the treatment is very similar to that found to be effective against the freshwater counterpart, *Ichthyophthirius multifiliis*, where the parasite is only vulnerable to medication during its free-swimming phase.

Velvet

Amyloodinium ocellatum is the culprit in this instance. The fish is covered with a very light dusting that gives it a velvety finish, hence the common name for this ailment. The gills may also be infected and the fish behaves with irritable restlessness, often dashing around and breathing rapidly.

Both *Cryptocaryon* and *Amyloodinium* can be successfully treated in a separate tank with long-term baths using proprietary remedies (usually copper-based). You may be advised to treat the fish with antibiotic-supplemented food afterwards as a protection against another outbreak from spores of the parasites that are still developing back in the main aquarium. If you have the resources of a spare tank, then keeping the main aquarium 'fish-free' for a few weeks may help to eradicate any remaining parasites; they die off unless they can find a host.

Hole-in-the-head

This unpleasant complaint is brought about by several factors: poor water conditions, vitamin deficiencies and a protozoan called *Octomita*

Right: This regal tang (Paracanthurus hepatus) *is suffering from the marine form of white spot disease, or marine 'ich', caused by the protozoan parasite* Cryptocaryon irritans. *The condition will respond to proprietary treatments. Always follow the maker's directions carefully.*

(Hexamita) necatrix. The 'holes' appear around the head and also along the lateral line. Obviously, improving the fishes' living conditions is beneficial, and providing a regular supply of high-quality, vitamin-rich (especially stabilised vitamin C and vitamin D) foods will also help. If herbivorous fish such as tangs are affected, some experts suggest that blanched or microwave-cooked broccoli constitute a successful remedy.

Pop eye

This is yet another 'painful-to-see' ailment that, again, can be helped by better water conditions and the passage of time. As the common name suggests

(only the most erudite use the scientific term *exophthalmia*!), one or both eyes protrude from the head as the result of a bacteria-induced swelling behind the eye. However, damage caused by careless handling may also be to blame, so take great care when using nets. You could also make a larger than normal water change, especially if you have been neglecting this duty for too long.

In the case of anemonefish, an alternative explanation for excess mucus production could be, the onset of an attack by the parasite *Brooklynella*. Treating this parasite with the same remedy as for *Amyloodinium* and *Cryptocaryon* will not be successful, as it is more vulnerable to formalin and malachite treatments.

Less common problems

Perhaps the ailments that cause the most distress – to the fishkeeper, as well as to the fish – are those that only produce external symptoms when the internal damage has advanced to such an extent that a remedy is not possible. Such ailments may be the result of internal parasites or diseases that affect the fishes' metabolism, internal organs or digestive system. In these cases there is very little to do except, perhaps, bring an end to the suffering by disposing of the fish as humanely as possible.

> ### Disposing of fish humanely
>
> *At some point in your fishkeeping career, you may find it necessary to dispatch a fish because of illness or old age. If a sick fish is beyond saving, the best thing is to dispose of it humanely. If you can bring yourself to do it, the quickest method is to sever the spinal cord behind the head with a sharp knife. Alternatively, obtain the fish anaesthetic MS222 from a veterinary surgeon or pharmacist and leave the patient in a solution of this for several hours. Never flush a fish down the lavatory, throw it on the floor or place it alive in the freezer. Freezing affects the capillary blood vessels just under the skin, causing the fish great pain before it loses consciousness.*

Above: Here, 'hole-in-the-head' disease (or HLLE – Head and Lateral Line Erosion) has unfortunately lived up to its descriptive name. Better aquarium conditions may well have prevented its outbreak occurring in the first place.

Excessive mucus

Sometimes, as a result of aggression, a fish picks up a wound, or it may bang against an aquarium rock or ornament and scratch itself. Generally, such wounds are soon covered with an excess of mucus, as the fish's protection system springs into action. However, before this can happen, there is an opportunity for secondary disease to set in, especially if conditions in the aquarium are not at their best. This is usually the case with 'finrot', which neatly describes the symptoms and yet is not in itself a disease.

Given the limitations on the number of fish that can be kept in the aquarium, it is important to give some thought to which species you are going to keep. Remember that at the outset you will be adding certainly not more than two or three fishes. Of course, you may already have mentally selected your favourites, but the criteria on which you base your choice are just as important as the choice of species.

At this early stage, it is a good idea to select inexpensive species. These are generally quite hardy, which means they are far more likely to survive your early attempts at keeping them, while not costing you too much financial heartbreak should things go wrong. A further interpretation of this rule is that, of course, the more exotic the fish, the more expensive and more delicate it is! However, the most important parameter at this, or any other, stage is always to buy healthy stock.

Choosing healthy fish

Always select brightly coloured fish, with well-defined (not smudged) colour patterns. They should be swimming purposefully, in full control of their movements, and able to position themselves at will at any depth of water. Bear in mind, too, the fishes' natural characteristics. For example, don't expect a fish that is normally active in the evening to be constantly active during daylight hours. It may well be resting while you are contemplating its purchase. Examine the fins for any obvious splits. The surface of the skin or scales should be free of spots, pimples or wounds. Although freshwater fishes swim with their fins folded when ailing, this is not a sign of ill-health in marine fishes. Many of them swim with folded fins as a matter of course. However tempted you are by any particular species, never ever buy fish from a tank containing sick or dead fish.

Be sure to find out from the dealer whether the fish is taking food readily. This is not quite the same as being reassured that it is being fed regularly; you should ask to see it being fed if you have any doubts. Most marine fishes die in captivity through the inability of their owners to provide them with the correct diet. (For feeding advice see pages 50-53.)

Left: When faced with the wide range of fishes to choose from at the aquatic store, you should know what to look for, so that you only buy healthy stock. Don't just buy fish you like the look of; they might not be compatible.

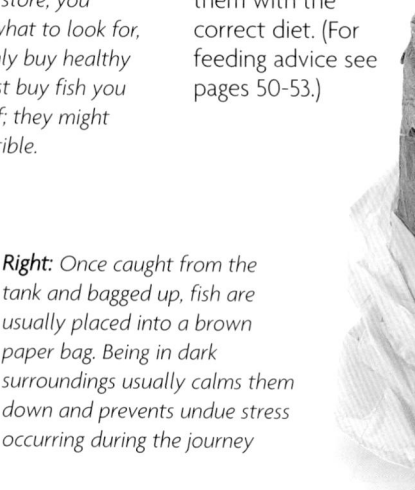

Right: Once caught from the tank and bagged up, fish are usually placed into a brown paper bag. Being in dark surroundings usually calms them down and prevents undue stress occurring during the journey

The fins and what they do

Marine fishes have the usual array of fins, although there are more variations to their shape than among freshwater fishes. As a prelude to the selection of marine fishes that follows on pages 62-73, here we consider the names of the fins and the role they play.

Dorsal fin
Acts like a keel to prevent the fish rolling as it swims. Some fish have two.

Right: *The cowfish (Lactoria cornuta) has a rigid body and an unusual arrangement of fins. The dorsal, anal and pectoral fins work as paddles and the caudal fin can close up like one of the horns. There are no pelvic fins. Not surprisingly, it swims fairly slowly.*

Caudal fin (tail)
Provides the initial thrust for forward motion.

Pectoral fins
For fine manoeuvring. All fish have two.

Anal fin
Stabilises the fish in the same way as the dorsal fin does.

Pelvic, or ventral fins
Help to stop the head pitching down. Most fish have two: some have none.

Buying healthy fish

Healthy marine fish have:
Clear eyes
Bright colours
Well-defined patterns
Robust bodies
Effortless swimming action
No spots, wounds, external growths or split fins
No breathing or positioning problems
Healthy appetites
Confident actions

Anemonefishes and damselfishes

Family: Pomacentridae

Members of the Pomacentridae family make excellent aquarium subjects. They have several very appealing characteristics for the marine fishkeeper: they are colourful, active and hardy, readily available and inexpensive. Who could want for more? Members of the anemonefish group are usually associated with sea anemones, amongst whose tentacles they find a safe home.

As they are more nitrate-tolerant than most species, these fishes are often the first to be introduced into the newly set-up aquarium, but this does not mean you can be any less rigorous in your preparations before introducing them.

 Maroon clown
Premnas biaculeatus

This is the largest of the anemonefishes, reaching about 17cm (6.6in), although males are usually smaller. It gets one of its popular names – clownfish – from its quaint swimming action, the other – the spinecheek anemonefish – from the very visible twin spines just below the eye. It may not be quite as dependent on a sea anemone as other members of the family.

▲ Fire clown
Amphiprion ephippium

The bold-feeding fire, or tomato, clown only conforms slightly to the usual 'white markings on a reddish body' family coloration. Only juveniles have a vertical thin white line passing down over their head, but this fades with age. The red-orange body is marked by an oval, dark-brown patch. All the fins are a plain red-orange colour, too.

The often territorial damselfishes do not depend on a sea anemone, preferring to find their sanctuaries amidst the branching coral heads much higher in the water level. Species in this segment of the family are in the size range 7-15cm (2.75-6in), with coloration embracing dark stripes, brilliant electric blues to sooty black. All members of the Pomacentridae are egg-depositors that guard their eggs much like freshwater cichlids.

▼ Humbug
Dascyllus aruanus

Dark and light contrasting colours are typical of the genus. This fish can be confused with D. melanurus, from which it can be distinguished by a black edge to the dorsal fin, but no black area across the rear of the caudal fin. This fish has a wide natural range.

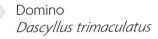

◀ Goldtail demoiselle
Chrysiptera parasema

The brilliant blue body has a touch more yellow to its posterior end than the many other similarly coloured damselfishes, which should make identification easier.

All damselfishes are territorial and quarrelsome and will pick on any new introductions into what they obviously consider as 'their' territory. To counter this behaviour, either introduce a small number of damselfishes at once or relocate the aquarium decorations so that everyone is too busy choosing new territories to pick a fight.

▶ Domino
Dascyllus trimaculatus

The three white spots on the jet black body are only found on juvenile forms and fade with increasing maturity, when coloration turns to a disappointing sooty grey with less distinct (if at all visible) white markings. Another feature of the juvenile's behaviour is its association with large sea anemones, a trait it loses as an adult, when it exhibits its congregational nature amongst the coral heads with others of its kind.

Angelfishes and butterflyfishes

Family: Pomacanthidae

In many angelfish species, the colour patterns of juveniles are totally different to that of the adults. A rearward-growing spine at the base of the gill cover distinguishes these fish from butterflyfish. The so-called dwarf species from the genus *Centropyge* require less living space than their larger relatives, whose specialist feeding habits often makes aquarium acclimatisation difficult.

▼ Cherubfish
Centropyge argi

The deep royal blue colour of the body extends into all the fins, except for the pectoral fins, which are bright yellow, as is the head. The eye and opercular spine are edged in bright blue. The cherubfish requires some green vegetable matter in its diet.

◁ Emperor angelfish
Pomacanthus imperator

The diagonal alternating stripes of blue and yellow make this fish very easy to recognise. The black mask over the eye and the upward-sweeping dark area immediately behind the gill-covers effectively break up the natural fish silhouette. The bright yellow dorsal and caudal fins only add to the exciting colours of this fish.

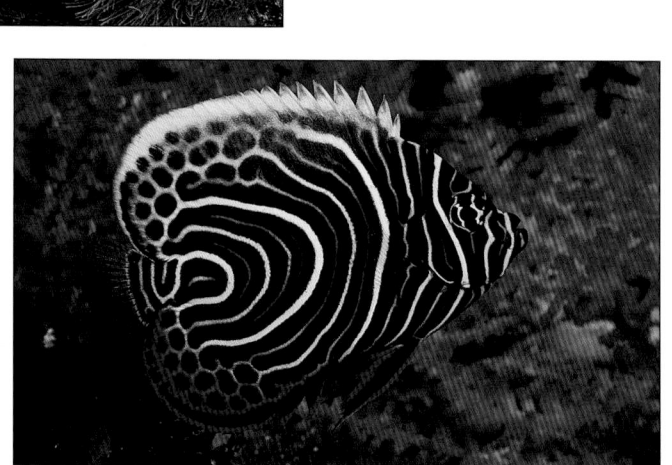

Right: In common with many juvenile angelfish forms, the juvenile emperor angelfish is quite different in coloration to the adult. In this species, the body is dark blue with white markings in a vaguely concentric pattern.

Yellow longnosed butterflyfish
Forcipiger longirostris

This species not only closely resembles its relative F. flavissimus, but also shares much of the same distribution area, from East Africa to Hawaii, Japan to Austral Island, including the Great Barrier Reef. However, F. longirostris has the longer snout and the steeper forehead, while F. flavissimus has a larger gape.

Despite their apparently specialised 'feeding equipment', longnoses make good aquarium subjects, as they will accept a wide variety of foods in captivity.

Family: Chaetodontidae

The butterflyfishes have oval bodies very similar to those of the angelfishes, but they use their more pointed snouts to explore coral and rock crevices for food. They are typically active during daylight hours, retreating amongst the coral heads at night. Very often, the true eye is hidden in a darker patch, with a false, decoy 'eye' elsewhere on the body to attract the attention of potential predators. Although several species are quite hardy and highly suited to aquarium life, there are other more spectacularly coloured species with feeding specialities that really ought to exclude them from consideration for the home aquarium.

Threadfin butterflyfish
Chaetodon auriga

The threadfin butterflyfish shares its 'herringbone' striped patterning of grey-black stripes on a silvery yellow background with two or three other relatives. The common name refers to a threadlike extension to the yellow rear portion of the dorsal fin. Although threadfins usually have an 'eye-spot' in the yellow area of the dorsal fin, some populations on the seaward side of reefs do not.

Wrasses, surgeonfishes and tangs

Family: Labridae

The numerous species of wrasse occur in all shapes and sizes and, once again, there is often a marked difference in coloration between juvenile and adult forms. Generally speaking, only juveniles are suitable for life in captivity. Most wrasses are constantly active in the aquarium and many lie on the substrate at night. Some spin a 'nightshirt' of mucus in which to pass the hours of darkness, while others bury themselves in the substrate.

Green birdmouth wrasse
Gomphosus coeruleus

The constantly active birdmouth wrasse has a curious swimming action that gives the impression that the fish is 'flying' through the water with a swooping action more reminiscent of a bird than a fish. The extended snout also resembles a bird's beak. The male fish (shown here) is green-blue, while the female is a dull brown.

Banana wrasse – *Halichoeres chrysus*

The brilliant yellow coloration and the shape of the body are responsible for this species' popular name. It has three black spots on the dorsal fin and one on the caudal peduncle to distinguish it from the similar-looking canary-top wrasse, H. leucoxanthus. In this species, only the top half of the body is yellow, while the lower half is silvery white.

Family: Acanthuridae

The identifying characteristics of the surgeons and tangs are oval bodies, steeply rising foreheads, erectile scalpels on the caudal peduncle and a decidedly herbivorous nature. The name 'tang' is derived from the German word 'seetang', meaning seaweed, which forms the fishes' staple natural diet. Not surprisingly, they appreciate a high proportion of vegetable matter in their diet in captivity. Many surgeons and tangs are finely decorated with brilliant colours and bizarre facial patternings.

Most are intolerant of their own kind, especially those with similar colours or body shapes, but in a large aquarium it is possible that oval shapes may coexist with the disc-shaped species without constant quarrelling.

▶ Yellow tang
Zebrasoma flavescens

This brightly coloured yellow fish can be distinguished from other all-yellow fishes, such as the lemonpeel angelfish (Centropyge flavissimus), herald's angelfish (C. heraldi) and even the related juvenile mimic surgeonfish (Acanthurus pyroferus), by its tall finnage and more laterally compressed body. It relishes vegetable matter and will happily munch on scalded lettuce leaves placed in the aquarium.

◀ Regal tang – *Paracanthurus hepatus*

This aquarium favourite is easy to identify by its royal blue body decorated with the familiar 'painter's palette' outline and the bright yellow caudal and pectoral fins. It depends heavily on well-oxygenated water and appreciates warmth. Like all members of this family, regal tangs can be territorially minded, so adequate tank space with plenty of retreats is called for.

Triggerfishes and basslets

Family: Balistidae

Triggerfish have two distinguishing physical characteristics: their pelvic fins are just rudimentary stubs and the first of their two dorsal fins is usually carried flat in a groove until the fish needs to erect it. When the fish feels threatened it can take defensive action by locking the dorsal fin into position using a releasable 'trigger' – the device that gives these fish their popular name.

▼ Clown triggerfish
Balistoides conspicillum

Disruptive colour patterning breaks up the body outline and camouflages the body in the constantly changing, dappled sunlit waters of the reef. The mouth is accentuated by a bright yellow surround and the teeth are very sharp; handle the fish with care. The clown triggerfish accepts all meaty foods, but will also attack invertebrates and aquarium hardware.

▲ Picasso triggerfish
Rhinecanthus aculeatus

With a native common name, Humu-humu-nuku-nuku-a-puaa, almost as bizarre as its colour patterning, this species always attracts attention. The yellow lips and elongated yellow line rearwards across the gill cover gives the impression of an immense gape; the rest of the colour patterning is indeed modern-surrealistic, as its attributed name implies.

Family: Serranidae

The basslets form what cynics might call the 'acceptable face' of the Serranidae family being, as they are, less malevolent-looking, of modest size and generally better-mannered in the aquarium. Many are secretive, cave-dwelling fish, constantly patrolling the rubble at the base of coral reefs not too far away from the security of their bolt-holes. Because of their size, there are no problems associated with disposing of their waste products, something that cannot be said for the related 'monsters of the deep.'

With their brilliant coloration, they make excellent subjects for the aquarium, especially for reef tanks, where they are quite compatible with invertebrates.

◀ Swiss guard basslet
Liopropoma rubre

This species, common in the waters of Florida, Yucatan and Venezuela, is a secretive species and not actually seen very often in nature. Its alternating stripes of reddish brown and yellow are reminiscent of the colours of the uniform of the Papal Swiss Guard in the Vatican City in Rome. It is often offered for sale, generally peaceful in the aquarium and eats all foods.

▲ Royal gramma
Gramma loreto

This brilliantly coloured fish comes from Western Atlantic and Caribbean waters, which it shares with the bicolor basslet (Liopropoma klayi), whose cerise colour is limited to the head region. However, it it is far more frequently confused with the royal dottyback (Pseudochromis paccagnellae), whose two similar colours are separated by a hardly discernible thin white line.

Blennies and gobies

Family: Blenniidae

The Blenniidae family would appear to offer a wide range of its modestly sized members for aquarium culture but, it must be said, not all are entirely suitable. While many spend their time peacefully scurrying around the substrate going about their business, others take advantage of their mimicry skills to predate on other fish as they imitate more benign species. For example, the sabre-toothed blenny (Aspidontus taeniatus) is a lookalike cleanerfish (Labroides dimidiatus), seeking a free mouthful of flesh from its victims rather than offering to remove parasites. A characteristic of many blennies is curly 'eyebrows', but all have double dorsal fins and blunt foreheads.

Smith's fang blenny
Meiacanthus smithi

This smart fish from the Maldives (and similar to another fang blenny, Plagiotremus phenax), has a smoky grey-blue body topped with a white-edged dark blue dorsal fin. The anal fin is blue. The black-streaked caudal fin is rounded and not lyre-shaped. This genus is far more adventurous than most blennies, as it is equipped with a fully functional swimbladder that allows it to venture up into midwater far more easily than its more substrate-bound relatives.

Bicolor blenny
Ecsenius bicolor

Generally, the forward half of the body is dark blue-brown with a bright yellow rear portion. The two sections of the continuous dorsal fin match the corresponding part of the body; anal and caudal fins are yellow. Variations in colour include an all-brown form or a dark-topped body with silvery blue lower flanks. When spawning, the male turns red with white transverse bars, the female yellow.

Family: Gobiidae

To many fishkeepers, gobies and blennies are an almost interchangeable group of fishes, sharing many behavioural characteristics. However, the distinguishing feature of members of the Gobiidae family is that the pelvic fins are usually fused (fully or partially) into a suction disk, which helps the fish to maintain its position on a firm surface.

Many species have very distinctive lifestyles. For example, they may live in substrate burrows in close association with invertebrates such as pistol shrimps. Like blennies, gobies make excellent aquarium subjects, demanding only modest-sized aquariums, yet offering a fascinating glimpse of marine life in return. Increasing numbers of gobies have been bred in captivity.

▼ Neon goby – *Gobiosoma oceanops*

The neon goby is rather shortlived, but is still one of the most popular aquarium fish. It makes an excellent aquarium subject, being hardy, easy to keep and breed. In the wild, it sits in crevices or caves waiting either for food or perhaps a customer for its cleaning services; it even 'cleans' divers' hands.

▲ Citron goby
Gobiodon citrinus

Unlike most gobies, the citron, or coral, goby is not a bottom-dwelling species. Instead, it spends its time among the branches of coral heads, protected against predation by a bitter-tasting mucus covering its skin.

Although the popular name implies a lemon yellow coloration, this species is variable in colour; green or brown specimens with red cheek stripes are males. Solid yellow animals are females. In fact, all individuals start life as females.

Miscellaneous marine species

▲ Longnosed hawkfish – *Oxycirrhites typus*

This species is not an active fish; it spends its time sitting on an outcrop of coral or any suitable aquarium decoration waiting for a feeding opportunity to present itself. While this apparently peaceful occupation may seem innocent enough, small fishes may be at risk. Tiny growths known as cirri are often seen at the tips of the dorsal spines and are responsible for the derivation of the family name, Cirrhitidae.

▼ Cowfish – *Lactoria cornuta*

The cowfish is covered with a suit of rigid bony plates. The only apparent area for growth is the part sticking out from the caudal peduncle. The fish gets its popular name from the 'horns' that project from the top of the square head. The convenient situation of the mouth right at the bottom corner of the head makes for easy substrate feeding. Cowfishes will accept almost all foods, including green foods, and appreciates shellfish. It flips them up with a jet of water from the mouth and catches them as they fall.

Banggai – *Pterapogon kauderni*

This silver-and-black fish, also known as the Borneo or highfin cardinalfish, is very reminiscent of the freshwater angelfish (Pterophyllum scalare). The large pelvic and anal fins mirror the two separate dorsal fins, while the whole body is overlaid with white dots (not a symptom of disease!)

The fish is very amenable to captivity and many public aquariums have bred them freely; they are mouthbrooders.

Decorated dartfish - *Nemateleotris decora*

While happy to hover in groups in midwater, where water currents bring their food, these stunning fish (also known as purple firefish) require immediate access to safe bolt-holes should they feel threatened. An aquarium suitably furnished with rocks is a prerequisite if these beautiful fishes are to settle down in captivity.

For the majority of the time that marine fishes have been kept in the aquarium, supplies of livestock have been provided by wild-caught specimens. The reason for this is not hard to see: the fish themselves are caught in relatively shallow waters and labour is inexpensive, both on the catching side and in the initial handling operations. Modern air transportation means that a larger proportion of fishes arrive alive and well, and their chances of survival in the aquarium are much greater than in the early days. Thus far, there has been no incentive for captive breeding, but nowadays there is a growing concern over the practice of denuding natural resources.

To take one example: the hugely appealing seahorse, with its unusual appearance and unique breeding behaviour, is under constant threat, not only from the aquarium trade, but also from Far Eastern souvenir manufacturers and practitioners of exotic medicine. Caring for this fish in captivity is hard enough as it is, and knowing that its wild stocks are under threat as a result of other demands means that something must be done to ensure its survival.

Another real anxiety concerns the practices employed to capture wild specimens. The greatest fear relates to the use of cyanide, which may make collection easier, but usually results in the release onto the market of much weakened fishes. As a consequence, even more fish are collected from the wild, thus denuding natural resources even further. Add to this a parallel cause for alarm over the collecting of coral, which also destroys the fishes' natural habitat in the process, and you have a true incentive to farm corals on an industrial basis or,

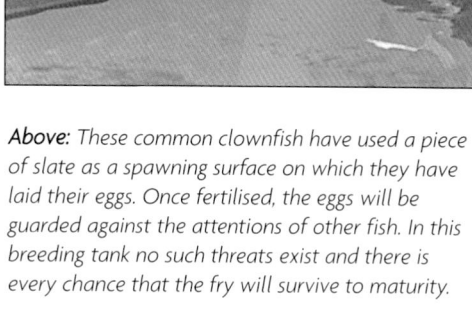

Above: These common clownfish have used a piece of slate as a spawning surface on which they have laid their eggs. Once fertilised, the eggs will be guarded against the attentions of other fish. In this breeding tank no such threats exist and there is every chance that the fry will survive to maturity.

Below: The seahorse has a unique method of breeding. Fertilised eggs are hatched in the male's abdominal pouch. The young fry may be hard to raise to maturity in a home marine aquarium.

alternatively, to develop realistic-looking replicas.

Due to their natural breeding behaviour, it is not possible to breed many of the marine species in captivity – not even in the largest public aquariums – so interest in captive breeding must be concentrated on those species that can be practicably reproduced.

Physical size and methods of breeding are the two main contributing factors to success. As many freshwater fishkeepers will know, there is always a risk of high egg losses when breeding egg-scattering species and similarly, in the marine aquarium, breeding successes have come from modestly sized species and those that deposit and care for their eggs. Such species include the anemonefish, damselfish, basslets, blennies, gobies, pipefish, seahorses, mandarinfish and the like. Several other genera may well spawn in the aquarium, but the real challenge lies in raising the fry to maturity; once again, feeding problems rear their ugly head. Most marine fish fry require planktonic-sized foods to begin with and it is the ability to produce sufficient quantities to meet their demands regularly (and reliably) that will 'crack the code.'

The reward for success will be much hardier species for the fishkeeper, with captive-bred specimens already acclimatised to aquarium life. The arrival of any substantial quantities of captive-bred fishes onto the market will also mean a reduction in prices and a continuing impetus for interest in marine fishkeeping for the foreseeable future. It is challenges such as this that face anyone willing to embrace the fascinating hobby of marine fishkeeping.

Right: Environments such as this will be less threatened, through over-fishing and over-collecting of corals, once captive breeding programmes become well established.

INDEX

Page numbers in **bold** indicate major entries; *italics* refer to captions and annotations; plain type indicates other text entries.

CREDITS

Practical photographs by Geoffrey Rogers
© Interpet Publishing. The publishers
would also like to thank the following
photographers for providing images,
credited here by page number and
position: B(Bottom), T(Top), C(Centre),
BL(Bottom Left), etc.

Aqua Press: 8(L), 9, 14(R), 19(L), 41(BL), 48,
49(T), 52(BL), 53, 56, 74(R), 75(M. Dune)
Dave Bevan: 67(R)
Bruce Coleman Collection: 8(R, Franco
Banfi), 40(Pacific Stock)
Les Holliday: 52(R), 74(C)
Jerrard Bros. plc (Arcadia): 41(TC)
Photomax (Max Gibbs): Title Page,
Copyright page, 6, 38, 47(TR), 49(B), 58, 59,
61(L, R), 62(L, R), 63(BL, TC, BR), 64(BL, TC,
BR), 65(L, R), 66(L, R), 67(L), 68(TL, BR), 69(L,
R), 70(T ,B), 71(T, B), 72(L, R), 73(L,R)
W A Tomey: 11(Mr. Boertje)

Artwork illustrations by Phil Holmes and
Stuart Watkinson © Interpet Publishing.

The publishers would like to thank
Maidenhead Aquatics Ascot Waterworld,
Country Gardens Garden Centre,
Windlesham, Surrey for providing
photographic facilities. Thanks are also due
to Heaver Tropics, Ash, Kent; RossLab plc.,
Gravesend, Kent and Swallow Aquatics,
Southfleet, Kent

The information and recommendations in
this book are given without any
guarantees on the part of the author and
publisher, who disclaim any liability with
the use of this material.